P9-BUH-481

KEETON

IN THE

KITCHEN

Rachel,

I hope you enjoy this book and make lots of delicious recipes!!

Eat well always!!

Shan

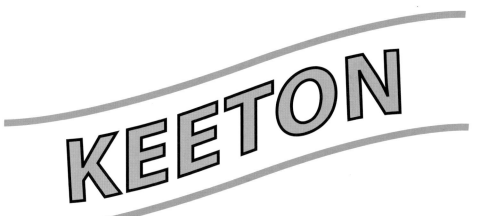

KEETON

IN THE
KITCHEN

*A Celebration
of Family,
Friends and Food*

SHAWN KEETON

Acclaim Press
MORLEY, MISSOURI

Acclaim Press
— Your Next Great Book —

P.O. Box 238
Morley, MO 63767
(573) 472-9800
www.acclaimpress.com

Design: Ron Eifert
Cover Design: M. Frene Melton

Copyright © 2010 Shawn Keeton

All Rights Reserved.

No part of this book shall be reproduced or transmitted in any form or by
any means, electronic or mechanical, including photocopying, recording
or by an information or retrieval system, except in the case of brief
quotations embodied in articles and reviews, without the prior written
consent of the publisher. The scanning, uploading and distribution of this
book via the Internet or via any other means without permission of the
publisher is illegal and punishable by law.

ISBN-10: 1-935001-62-0
ISBN-13: 978-1-935001-62-1

Library of Congress Control Number: 2010913776

First Printing: 2010
Printed in the United States of America
10 9 8 7 6 5 4 3 2 1

Contents

Dedicated to my wonderful
loving family;

without you, this wouldn't
have been possible.

IN THE
KITCHEN

*A Celebration
of Family,
Friends and Food*

The Beginning

It's really hard to say where it all began. Now, I'm not talking about how "it" all began as in the "it" of the entire world, life on earth, the realization of intelligence and that entire phenomenon. The "it" to which I am referring is the appreciation (and truth be known downright love affair) that I have with food.

Now, before I go any further I know some of you are thinking to yourselves, what qualifications does this guy have to talk about love? How would he know true love from au gratin potatoes? The answer is simple. I am a foodaholic, a full blown food junkie. I am a man who appreciates food and wine in the same way and with the same zeal that some people love their automobiles, their homes and even their vacation destinations. I LOVE FOOD. It couldn't really be any simpler than that. I love all types of food from all types of places, which I will get into later in this book, but now back to the beginning.

When I started this project, I wanted to write a cookbook that was different than other selections comfortably resting on your nearby bookstore shelves. I, as I'm sure do many of you, have shelves full of cookbooks. Some are easy to read and the recipes are easy to duplicate, while others require having a PhD in Foodology to decipher and four kitchens worth of utensils to prepare. Occasionally I look at those books, but rarely do I attempt to make something out of them. Usually my attempts are undone by not having a pinch of Mongolian Yak Dung on hand, and the entire concoction suffers the ill-fate of being ruined because of the lack of strange items in my kitchen. I am of course satirizing to a point, but hopefully you are shaking your head in agreement with the realization that my point is a common one for many people.

Cookbooks tend to fit like blue jeans. You have a few that fit really well and get worn to the point of having holes in them. There are a few other pairs that fit decently but are only worn around the house occasionally; they are then put back into the closet with the wonderful thoughts of, "maybe when I lose some weight they will fit better." Then you have the ones that you only wear when you are weed-eating. Possibly they are worn on days that don't end in "y." They sit idly by, glaring at you from the shelf. "You can't make me," the recipes scream from the pages, much as the jeans say, "I am not fitting around that butt." It's impossible to get rid of them, as that little devil sitting on your shoulder keeps convincing you that they really are your friends. Well, my friends, I am here to say that these cookbooks are not your friends.

In essence, these cookbooks seem to be a microcosm of life in general. They tend to be our unattainable food goal, but one that we hang onto just in case. The books I am referring to are the ones that have the great looking pictures of the extravagant recipes that all have 36 ingredients and require 9 hours of prep time and 6 hours of cooking in a convection style oven that less than 1% of homes actually own. That doesn't stop us from gazing through the pages with unadulterated excitement, attempting in every way to convince ourselves that tomorrow night that's going to be our dinner, come hell or high water. It is going to happen! We just know it is. It is a great plan on paper. The problem exists in the actual preparation of these intricate and time consuming recipes. We lack the resources, availability of ingredients, technical knowledge and all the other things that make it possible to prepare dishes of that magnitude. Now don't get me wrong. I am not saying even for one second that should we set our minds to doing it, that it wouldn't be possible. I'm simply saying that with the rigors of daily life gouging us in the ribs every two seconds, it's not happening any time soon. This reality is really what pushed me to write this cookbook. Well, that and the fact that everyone I know says I should write a cookbook. I began to feel like some sort of a failure since I didn't have a cookbook already. I didn't want it to be a run of the mill, "you've read it fifty times already" book. I wanted it to be different, fun, easy, exciting (which truly begs the question of whether a cookbook can be exciting) and more. I wanted the book to be a reflection of my life and my experiences with food and its preparation.

Experience is really a good word for that description. I think all cooking is about experiences and, in essence, the true life blood of what brings us together as families and friends. If you think about it, some of the most important and certainly cherished moments in our lives are based around food. Holiday dinners come to mind. It's a celebration of family, but it's also about food. No one wants to keep going to someone's house if the food stinks. I know, I've been in that situation many times. Good food typically equates to good times. In addition to holidays we gather at barbecues, after graduations and marriages. Heck, we even gather and eat after funerals. That may be a tad morbid to say, but you see my point. The celebrations of life revolve around food. Preparing it and serving it can truly affect the outcome of the gathering, both good and bad. The question then becomes how do we get the food to live up to the expectations that we have for it? I will answer that question later on, however, now it's back to the beginning.

I'm pretty sure that upon being born my mother and father loaded my bottle with heavy cream and blueberry sauce reductions. I have to feel like there's a pretty good chance that is the case, after all, how could anyone love heavy cream as much as I do without having been subjected to it as an infant? Oddly enough, I live in a blueberry-less state for the most part and blueberries are my favorite fruit, further circumstantial evidence of my food upbringing. I will say that after suffering from injuries in a serious car accident in 1984, I don't really recall that much of my childhood, so I could be wrong about not knowing my food upbringing. There's a book out that basically puts forth the idea that all things are cataloged in your brain, its just that some are easier to recall than others. Perhaps I should see one of those hypnotic people and have them look deep into the darkest regions of my brain to find all the food history and bring it forth. If it weren't for the fact that my arteries might remember all the cholesterol, I would go there. I do know this: from the time I was little, I have had a passion for food, a pure passion that has developed over the years into a drive to learn every technique, every style, every preparation that I can. It's become an obsession in some ways. I want to know, I want to taste, and I want to teach.

All those things being as they are, I wanted this book to rest upon a foundation. In many ways things are much easier to grasp if you understand where they came from. It's like shooting a basketball. You build a foundation of arc, trajectory, and other basics, and the end result becomes easier to fathom. Instead of just throwing a bunch of wonderful, tasty and easy to prepare recipes on the pages with an occasional picture, I wanted to build a framework of how I came by these ideas. If I let you in on the "why" and the "how," perhaps the "I'm and now" will come easier to you. This book won't become the jeans that make your butt feel like three quarter pounders just settled into it, more it will be the sleek skinny jeans that everyone notices, especially your significant other. I can't really preach family, friends and food if I can't deliver on making those times a better all around experience. Maybe I can and maybe I can't, but I am certainly going to try to take you for a culinary ride and hopefully by the end our hair (more yours than mine seeing as how I have very little left) will need to be combed and our bellies will be full of the delicious knowledge.

My Cooking Start

Now before I go any further, I must admit that I have been a very lucky fellow. All the while I was growing up (my wife would say I am still in the process of growing up), I was around people, actually women, who were good cooks. I am not sure if it was a faux pas in those days, but like many others I was not around many men who cooked. I grew up primarily in a farming/small town environment, so mostly it was men at work and women cooking. It truly is funny when I look back on those days. It was a different time. Even today I find my son rolling his eyes when I tell him about buying chips for fifteen cents a bag or sodas for a quarter. Sometimes I wonder if I believe it myself, especially after going to the store and seeing the prices of today's items. Getting back to my original point though, I was subjected to great food and great cooking at an early age. I wasn't telling a lie when I said that I don't remember that much about my childhood, but I do remember bits and pieces of the food and the preparation techniques that my mother, stepmother and grandmothers used in their kitchens.

The first thing that comes to mind from back in those days is that most everything was fried or cooked in a skillet. If I had to rate the single biggest difference from back then (back then being the early 70's) until now it would be cooking techniques. I can hardly remember a time back in the days when food was grilled, stirfried in a wok or broiled. I'm sure there were times but it was a time of primarily frying and baking. If it couldn't be fried or baked it wasn't worth messing with. Being from Kentucky, that is still the case in many ways. Having traveled all around the world I can say without fail that no matter where you go on this planet if you say you're from Kentucky the first thing people say is fried chicken. Frying food is synonymous with living here. Even with the focus on not eating trans-fats, eating healthier and so on, it's still a way of life for many. Frankly, I love fried foods just as much as ever.

Fry Dredge
A key component to any fried meal.

1 cup flour
1 cup corn meal
1 tablespoon garlic
1 tablespoon Cajun seasoning
1 teaspoon black pepper
1 teaspoon chili powder

Mix all ingredients. For oysters or fish simply dredge and fry.
For veggies, soak them in water or milk for a few minutes before dredging.
Prep time: 15 minutes.

The great thing about this dredge is that it's very versatile. I use it on everything from wild turkey bites to broccoli. It's easy to make, can be made in bulk, at very little expense, and stores forever if you put it in a container with a tight-fitting lid. Usually when I make the dredge I do so in 5 to 10 pound increments. By doing that I now have fry dredge pre-made for fish fries, vegetable dustings and a great base of seasoned flour that has uses in many dishes beyond simply submerging them in hot oil. Don't underestimate the power of this dredge to bring roasts, fish, briskets and other things that you bake to another level.

Before I go any further I want to say this: in many of the cooking classes I have taught, one of the comments I most often get is "I don't like this or that." For instance someone will say (and has),

"I don't like garlic, so I won't make the dredge." In every recipe I put on these pages there is free licensing. What I mean by that is anything you like or don't like can be added or subtracted without effecting the overall dish unless its one of the main ingredients. Notice the word "main" in there: if it's a chicken dish and you decide to leave out the chicken it will effect the end product. If it's a chicken dish and you decide to leave out a clove of garlic, you will still end up with a chicken dish. Use your own judgment when it comes to this, but don't automatically assume you won't like something because it contains one or two small amounts of something you don't really like.

So now that you've got your fry dredge worked up, it's time to dunk some things. One of the first things I can say about dredging and frying almost anything is that it can be frustrating as heck to bread it up and fry it, only to have the breading fall off in the skillet. I know there are more than a few of you out there shaking your heads in agreement. It's frustrating and it's embarrassing to a degree, especially when you are serving the food and not just eating it yourself. There will be a few tips for this in the last section of the book.

Now that you're frying, let's look at some things that go great in the oil. The first of course is chicken. I love fried chicken, although I don't make it at home all that much. When cooked in good oil and using the above fry dredge in an iron skillet, fried chicken is one of my favorite things. Try to leave the skin on while frying it, as it keeps the moisture in better and allows the outside to crisp up nicely. Don't turn it too often, as this can lead to the breading coming loose as well. Beyond breaded food, I like to skillet fry lots of things such as:

Fried Taters and Onions

This is one of my all-time favorite foods.

4 large baking potatoes
1 large onion (sweet if available) cut into ¼" rings
1 small red pepper, roughly chopped
Seasoned salt (see recipe)
4 tablespoons grated Parmesan
¾ cup grated sharp cheddar
5 tablespoons butter

Microwave the potatoes on high for 12 minutes or until almost cooked though. You want them to be a little tough in the center. Remove them and, using a kitchen towel or heatproof glove, slice them ¼" thick. In a large skillet over medium high heat melt the butter and add the onions and peppers. Add the potatoes and allow to cook for 3 minutes before turning. Using a large spatula (or a small one if that's all you have), flip the mixture over and cook for an additional 3 to 4 minutes or until onions cook to your desired level. Sprinkle with the cheeses and serve immediately. Prep time: 15 minutes. Servings: 4.

The great thing about microwaving the potatoes is that it really speeds up the final product. If you want to fry the potatoes instead of microwaving, slice them and cook in the skillet 8 to 10 minutes prior to adding the onions and peppers. For the seasoned salt:

All Purpose Seasoned Salt

Makes a great all purpose shake.
I put this on EVERYTHING, from veggies to eggs.

½ cup salt
2 teaspoons black pepper
½ teaspoon garlic powder
½ teaspoon onion powder

¼ teaspoon cayenne pepper
½ teaspoon Italian seasoning

Mix all ingredients and put in a salt shaker. I make this up in larger quantities and keep a shaker full at all times. When you select a shaker to keep this in, make sure you pick one with larger holes. Most salt shakers don't have holes large enough to let all the delicious goodness of this out, so select carefully.
Prep time: 5 minutes.

At times I use another shake, one that fits better with foods that tend to be a little bland or need some pepping up:

Seasoned Shake

This one has a little more kick and if you don't like spicy, go easy.

½ cup coarse salt
¼ cup smoked paprika
¼ cup ground black pepper
½ tablespoon cayenne pepper
½ tablespoon garlic powder

Mix all ingredients and store in a sealed plastic bag out of direct sunlight.
Prep time: 5 minutes.

Obviously I make a lot of things in bulk to simply have them on hand. It sure beats scrambling to whip something up as people are walking through the door, which keeps the stress level at a minimum; it also saves money as I can buy these things in large quantities. Not to be understated, saving money keeps my wife happy, which in turn keeps me happy and so our entire household is happy. Now that we have the skillet hot, let's see what else we can cook up. Here's another recipe from when I was a wee tot that really sticks out to me. I named it my best, even though it was really my mom's best burger recipe. I don't think she will mind:

My Best Burgers

These easy burgers are a pan-fried home run.

2 lbs. 90/10 ground beef
1 cup shredded Parmesan cheese
½ cup shredded sharp cheddar cheese
3 teaspoons Worcestershire sauce
1 teaspoon hot sauce (optional)
½ teaspoon garlic powder
½ teaspoon onion powder
1 teaspoon ground black pepper with smoke flavor
½ teaspoon coarse salt

Preheat a large skillet to medium or start charcoals in time for them to be gray before adding meat. Mix all ingredients in a large bowl and pat into 1" thick burgers. Place in skillet and cook for approximately 6 minutes per side, flipping once. If you are placing them over charcoals or on an indoor grill put them several inches from the heat and only turn after 6 to 7 minutes. Prep Time: 10 minutes. Servings: 8.

Boy, my mouth is watering like crazy thinking about those juicy, tasty burgers. For an extra special treat, place a chopped onion and several chopped mushrooms in the skillet after you have removed the burgers and cook them for 3 to 4 minutes. Serve over toasted buns. So now that the arteries are sticking together with all the fried food, let's talk for a second about frying equipment. Actually, let me stick this little diamond in here before we get to frying equipment:

Pan Seared Chicken with Fresh Tarragon

A real hit at the cooking classes.

4 large skinless, boneless chicken breasts
4 sprigs fresh Tarragon
1 tablespoon butter
1 cup dry white wine
1 bunch green onions, chopped
1 pint heavy cream
3 tablespoons chopped Tarragon leaves

Heat a skillet over medium heat. Cut slits across the chicken breasts (not cutting all the way through) about ½" apart. Place several Tarragon leaves in each slit. Put the butter in the skillet and, once it's melted, add the chicken. Sear the chicken for 5 to 6 minutes per side or until cooked through and juices run clear. Remove and set aside. Add the wine and green onions to the skillet. Bring to a boil and simmer for 2 minutes. Reduce heat and add cream. Boil gently for a minute or until the sauce has thickened. Stir in the chopped Tarragon, spoon over the chicken and serve.
Prep time: 30 minutes. Servings: 4.

Most everyone has a skillet, be it a big one or a small one, and most skillets can be adapted to fry most anything if given some thought. I prefer a heavy bottomed skillet for most frying (the exception being quick frying foods like eggs) as it heats more evenly and disperses the heat better. The key to frying is to sear the outside and thus lock in flavors and moisture.

Another key to frying is good oil. Back in the good old days of no one caring about cholesterol, lard was the preferred frying medium. I must confess that I still love foods fried in lard, and it holds up very well to sustained high temperatures. Let's say you are frying several pieces of chicken and they won't all fit in your skillet at the same time, forcing you to fry them in batches. In this situation you need an oil that will hold up to high temperatures for longer periods of time. For those of you who have fried whole turkeys, you know that the recommendation is peanut oil. Peanut oil can hold up to 350 degrees or more for the long periods of time that it takes to fry something as big as a turkey without scorching and turning black. If you used vegetable oil for instance, you run the risk of your oil smoking and becoming bitter. Always choose good quality oil and research the types of oils to see what will be the best for frying the things that you like to cook. What I mean is this: if you only fry chicken, find the oil and skillet that best fries chicken. This comes easily enough with just a little time spent in the kitchen. As with most of this book the key here is to try things and find what works. Keep in mind that lots of very good recipes come from trial and error, and in my case a lot of errors.

Let's move out of fried foods and my younger years now and get into the formative culinary times.

Japan or Bust

When I was 15 years old, and mostly a man, I embarked on a journey as a cultural exchange student to Sapporo, Japan. Now, before I go even one step into the wonderful food traditions and lifestyles of the Japanese people, you have to understand a few things. I was 15 years old. I was also a small town fella who had never lived in a city. In addition to being 15 years old, I was also six feet tall, a full six inches taller than most of the people I would be around. I was blond in a country of dark haired people, and I had gotten to the point when a man realizes for certain that girls really are cool. As a matter of fact, the raging hormones do everything possible to convince you that girls are the single coolest thing on the planet, and trust me, there are lots of cool things on the planet when you are 15 years old. Now, you may be wondering what this has to do with a cookbook. In writing this book I wanted to convey these recipes and their context in my life and experiences. I feel almost certain that if I had gone to Japan after puberty my food experiences would be far more in depth. It's very difficult to notice food when girls are in the room. As a matter of fact, they don't even have to be in the room. Usually they just need to be in the same zip code and they find their way in the brain of a 15-year-old boy. Beyond girls, the food experiences of Japan were awesome.

First and foremost, they are big time seafood eaters. Living on an island will tend to do that, I guess. It just so happens I am a big seafood guy as well. A recipe that I love to make is:

Panko Breaded Fish

Panko, the new flour.

1 lb. firm fish fillets (cod, catfish or the like)
1 cup buttermilk
2 cups seasoned flour
2 cups Panko Bread Crumbs (these are readily available
    Japanese Bread Crumbs)
Oil for frying
Salt and pepper to taste

Heat oil in a large skillet over medium high heat. You don't want the oil to smoke, but you want it very hot. Place the flour in a large plastic bag, add fillets a few at a time, and shake to coat. Pour buttermilk into a large bowl. Remove the fillets from the bag and place in the buttermilk, and then roll the fillets in the Panko Bread Crumbs. Place in the hot oil and cook for approximately 4 minutes per side (until they are well-browned) then flip. When the fillets are crisp and flaky, remove and place on a plate covered with paper towels (to drain). Sprinkle with salt and pepper.
Prep time: 10 minutes. Servings: 4.

Here we see the fabulous Panko Bread Crumbs. There may be no bigger fan of Panko Bread Crumbs in the world than me: I love the crunch, the flavor and the appearance that they give to food. If you are not sure what I am talking about, it's typically the breading found on tempura fried foods. If you are wondering what tempura fried foods are, we are in trouble because I can't explain it really. Very crunchy, golden brown breading that just loves to stick to food and make it ultra tasty. The great thing about Panko is that it's available in most every grocery store. Heck, even the groceries in my small town carry it. Try it on vegetables, fish, chicken and most anything you can fry and not ruin in the process. If you're wondering why this wasn't under the fried food section, I can only say this: just because. That reasoning seems to work with my son occasionally, so I will use it here as well. As I said, I am a big seafood guy. When I am cooking outdoors one of the dishes my family and I love is:

Grilled Salmon with Butter Cream Sauce

*Make an entire meal on the grill when you pair this
with the Grilled Veggies recipe.*

**1 medium salmon fillet, skin on
2 medium lemons, cut into ¼" slices
1 pint heavy cream
4 tablespoons salted butter
2 sprigs fresh dill, finely chopped
1 teaspoon cornstarch
4 tablespoons water
Seasoned shake to taste (see recipe)**

Season meat side of fillet with seasoned shake. Place lemon slices on meat. Place fillet on a medium hot grill, skin side down. Meanwhile in a small sauce pan heat cream and butter until hot, but do not boil. Add dill to sauce pan. Grill fillets for 8 to 10 minutes or until fish becomes opaque and flakes easily. In a small bowl combine cornstarch and water. Add to cream sauce a little at a time, stirring well between additions until desired consistency is reached. Remove salmon to a serving plate. Remove and discard lemon slices. Ladle cream sauce over meat and serve. Prep time: 10 minutes. Servings: 4.

Most any fish can be used in this recipe if you don't have access to salmon. If you are going to use very thin or very flaky fish, such as tilapia, you will need to place it on a double thickness of foil to keep it from falling through the grates. In addition to fish, this also works well over other seafood such as shrimp and scallops. Since I just mentioned scallops, I will drop this little beauty out there:

Pan Seared Scallops

My all time favorite seafood recipe.

1 lb. sea scallops
4 cloves garlic, minced or finely chopped
4 tablespoons butter
¼ cup green onions, chopped
Salt and pepper to taste

Heat a large skillet over medium high heat. Add the butter and garlic. Stir well. Add the scallops and cook for 2 minutes. Turn and add onions. Cook for another 2 minutes or until scallops are opaque. Serve over rice or thin spaghetti.
Prep time: 5 minutes. Servings: 4.

The great thing about this recipe is that you just made a wonderful-tasting, eye-pleasing dish that literally took a few minutes, plus whatever time your side dishes took. While it's on my mind, I'm going to go ahead and say, time spent in preparation is not always indicative of how the final product will turn out. There have been many times when I've spent hours in the kitchen preparing something that didn't look or taste any better than this scallop recipe. Recipes like this are great on weeknights when time is short. Always in the back of my mind is the thought that no matter how long I've spent, if it tastes good, it has been a success.

The Grilling Age

Once I got back from Japan and finally got a grip on what was going on inside my body, I started to focus more on food and preparations. Now mind you that wasn't easy, but having a steady girlfriend helped. The pervading thoughts of what I might lose anatomy-wise should I think about another woman kept me on the straight and narrow. That certainly aided my explorations into cooking in general but more specifically outdoor cooking, one of my real passions culinarily speaking.

There are many great things about grilling, not the least of which is that it usually involves having family or friends over. In a lot of ways grilling is synonymous with entertaining. When the grill or smoker is fired up you can almost smell the love. Seriously, the next time you light the grill or charcoal take a deep breath. I can almost assure you, your heart will be filled with love. Also note, it's best to do this before you actually cook anything; that way if you mess something up it doesn't get in the way of the love that's flowing.

A recipe or two ago we touched on grilling fish, which I honestly think is the most overlooked food when it comes to outdoor cooking. Steak, chicken and pork get all the publicity, and yet very few foods take to grilling any better than fish and seafood. One recipe I always think of when we are entertaining is:

Grilled Summer Veggies

A great way to use the bounty from your garden!

1 medium zucchini, roughly chopped
1 medium onion, roughly chopped
1 medium yellow squash, roughly chopped
4 tablespoons butter (margarine will work, but butter
  is better)
½ teaspoon seasoned salt
½ teaspoon pepper
6 slices bacon
2 tablespoons Worcestershire sauce

Double layer a large piece of aluminum foil. Spray with non-stick spray. Layer bacon slices on foil in a single layer. Layer on chopped veggies. Cut butter into several chunks and place on top. Sprinkle with salt and pepper and drizzle with Worcestershire sauce. Close foil and grill or bake on medium (350 degrees) for 25 minutes. Open and serve from packet. One thing I like to add is a tablespoon of bacon fat, just for additional flavor.
Prep time: 15 minutes. Servings: 4.

I love the simplicity of grilled vegetables, and boy are they delectable. Also on the plus side, they utilize vegetables that are in abundance in the summer, especially if you or someone you know has a garden. Every year when we are planting our garden we end up over planting zucchini and yellow squash. I can assure you that next year I will say to my wife, "This year I'm only planting a couple of each." Low and behold I will set 10 mounds of each and feel totally guilty when I can't use all of them. It's the starving kid in other countries thing that always leads to my guilt. The point is, it just seems like I should attempt to do so, or more simply that I should just plant less of them. That won't be the case however, so I will simply continue feeling bad about it and grilling what I can. While my grill is good and hot, I should say that one of the very first things that I learned to cook on a grill was:

Goobey Taters

A perfect side dish for steaks or burgers!

4 large potatoes cut into ¼" slices
1 large onion
2 tablespoons Worcestershire sauce
3 strips bacon
Salt and pepper

Double layer a large sheet of aluminum foil. Place bacon on foil.
Next, layer potatoes and onions. Pour Worcestershire sauce over
and season with salt and pepper. Seal aluminum foil and place on
medium hot grill for 20 minutes or until tender.
Prep time: 15 minutes. Servings: 4.

I'm sure you're wondering about that catchy title. Perhaps I
used World's Best or My Best too often, you're thinking. No, that's
not it. In actuality, it's the nickname of the guy who taught me
that recipe. Recipes for me tend to be like that. Oftentimes a great
idea or improvement simply comes from doing something that
someone else has already done and just changing it a bit to fit your
tastes better. Brand new recipes tend to be hard to come by. Most
all are simply additions or subtractions to existing ideas, mostly
due to the fact that very few "new" ingredients are being discov-
ered. Think about it for a minute: herbs, spices, salts and peppers
have been around for thousands of years. Fruits and vegetables
were being harvested and eaten by cavemen, as were most if not all
animal species. Instead of beginning anew, I believe food evolves.
One thing that I evolved to start grilling back in the 80's was:

Zucchini Boats with Tomato Gravy and Ground Chicken

Serve this recipe with a side salad and some crusty bread.

4 medium zucchini
1 small onion, chopped
1 15½ oz. can tomato sauce
1 6 oz. can tomato paste
3 teaspoons fresh basil, chopped
2 teaspoons fresh oregano, chopped
1 lb. ground chicken
1 cup shredded cheddar cheese + ¼ cup reserved
½ teaspoon seasoned salt
½ teaspoon black pepper

Slice zucchinis in half length wise. Carefully slice the centers out of the halves, leaving ½" around the edges. Roughly chop the centers into ½" cubes. Brush the insides of the "boats" with olive oil. Place on a medium hot grill for 8 minutes (or into a 250 degree oven for 20 minutes) or until slightly tender, and remove from grill. Meanwhile brown the ground beef, onions and centers of zucchinis in a skillet until burger is no longer pink. Drain. In a medium saucepan mix herbs, tomato sauce and tomato paste and bring to a boil. Simmer for 15 minutes. Mix sauce with ground meat and cheese. Fill the centers of the boats with the meat mixture. Top with remaining cheese. Bake at 350 for 20 minutes or until cheese is melted and bubbly.
Prep time: 20 minutes. Servings: 4.

Once again this is a recipe that I make often during the summer that utilizes available vegetables and herbs. Before I go on, don't jump to the conclusion that I only grill during the summer. Oh contraire mon frère, I grill just as much or more during the winter when it's cold out and there's nothing much else going on. Investing in a magnetic grill light really pays dividends here, as it gets dark before most of us get home from work. One real key to grilling is knowing the look and feel of how a dish should be. I can press on meat and tell if it's done to the consistency that I want because I have done it so many times before. In addition to that, I have learned over time how my grill and smoker cook, what I can expect as a finished product and how long that should take. It's no different than a stove or oven, once you do it a few times you can predict with good accuracy what it will take the next time. I could write an entire book on just grilling and smoking (and maybe one day I will). I'm focusing here on an all-around cookbook, therefore I'm going to lay out, in bare bones, a couple of my favorite recipes for making homemade marinade and barbecue sauce. Never again, unless you just happen to not have these ingredients, will you need to change your mind on a dish simply because you don't have a bottle of sauce on hand. A very easy to make sauce is:

Homemade Barbeque Sauce

Save money on barbeque sauce by making your own.

2 cups ketchup
2 teaspoons brown sugar
½ teaspoon salt
½ teaspoon black pepper
½ teaspoon garlic powder
½ teaspoon mustard

Mix all ingredients in a large saucepan over medium heat. Bring to a simmer, reduce heat and simmer for 10 minutes. Remove from heat, allow to cool, and refrigerate for at least one hour. Best if made early and allowed to set overnight. If you want it to be sweeter, add another teaspoon of brown sugar. This is especially good if you are using the sauce on ribs, which take on a sweeter sauce better than some other meats. (It also makes a very good sloppy joe sauce. Brown 1 pound of ground beef, 1 medium onion and 1 green pepper in a skillet and add sauce.) Prep time: 10 minutes.

See how easy that was? Simple and delicious and made with ingredients most people have around the house on days that end in "y." Experiment with that some by adding coarse ground or garlic mustard in place of standard yellow if you feel a little adventurous. If the mood really smacks you in the gut while you and the Misses (or Mister, according to your preference) are getting your grill time on, add a few dashes of your favorite hot sauce. I mean really, what says loving like spicy barbecue sauce. So let's say you got a little off your rocker and made that baby rock. The next time your grilling out, all hell has broken loose in your gut, you're rockin' like a palm tree in a hurricane and you are just not going to settle for anything less than MEGA BLASTER sauce, try this on for size:

Mom's Best Barbeque Sauce

Best if used soon after making. Does not keep well.

2 cups ketchup
2 teaspoons brown sugar
4 strips bacon
½ teaspoon salt
½ teaspoon black pepper
½ teaspoon garlic powder
1 small sweet onion, finely chopped
½ cup bourbon

Preheat a large skillet over medium heat. Add bacon and fry until crisp. Remove bacon. Add onions and sauté until browned. Add all other ingredients and bring to a simmer. Continue to simmer for 3 minutes. Remove from heat and baste on meat.
Prep time: 10 minutes.

Whooooooo weeee, boy are we kickin' this baby now. Rock on dudes and dudettes is all I can say when it comes to whiskey sauce. Keep in mind that the rockin' is all in your brains as the alcohol cooked out of it while it was simmering, but boy, when you hit any age past 35 it sure feels good to get crazy, liquor or not. Notice that recipe says "Mom's." Yep, that's my mom's recipe, and boy does it rock. Try it over:

Slow Smoked Ribs
Better than your favorite rib joint!

1 rack pork spare ribs
½ cup olive oil
2 teaspoons brown sugar
1 teaspoon chipotle powder
½ teaspoon garlic powder
½ teaspoon black pepper
½ teaspoon smoked salt
½ teaspoon onion powder

Heat a smoker (or oven) to 240 degrees. Mix the sugar, powders, salt and pepper. Coat the ribs well with the olive oil. Generously coat ribs on both sides with the rub, pressing it down into the meat. Most times the rack of ribs will need to be cut in half to properly fit in small smokers or in the oven. Cook uncovered for 4 hours adding apple or hickory chips once or twice during cooking, remove from heat, wrap in foil tightly and return to heat for 45 minutes. Remove and cover with a towel until ready to serve.
Prep time: 15 minutes. Servings: 3.

WOW, if ever there were a recipe that lived up to the old saying, "slap yo mamma for not makin it for ya," that's it. Those ribs come out tender, juicy and mighty delicious. When you top them with that sauce, it's enough to get you arrested in four states. A quick tip for ribs, especially if you don't have hours to slow cook them: place the ribs in a pressure cooker and cook according to the directions on the cooker. Remove from the slow cooker and place on a medium hot grill 4 minutes per side. Slather on sauce and serve. The first time I did this I blew my pressure cooker sky high. I can say with no uncertainty what-so-ever that burnt ribs dripping from the ceiling after a pressure cooker blew up is one of the worst smells to attempt to clear from a house. I smelled those burnt piggy sides for weeks after that. The mistake that I made was cooking the ribs in the pressure cooker for about 10 minutes. In a fit of goofy I decided to check them. When they weren't ready (which I should have known they wouldn't be) I simply put the lid back on and got the cooker back to rolling. All in good fun right? Well, yes and no. Once I opened the lid the moisture escaped. I then put the lid back on and got it back up to temperature without adding any more water. Soon enough they were burnt to the bottom and the cooker exploded due to no liquid. I'm assuming that's what it was; I was too mesmerized by the dripping froth of what had once been pork to know what really happened. Back to the whiskey for a second, for a great (and I mean great) fish marinade. Prior to grilling, try this:

Whiskey Marinade

From the home of the world's best bourbon, Kentucky!

½ cup whiskey or bourbon
½ cup olive oil
½ cup lemon juice
1 teaspoon fresh snipped dill
¼ teaspoon fresh ground black pepper
¼ teaspoon hot sauce
Sprinkle of coarse salt

Mix all ingredients in a non reactive bowl (see tip number 20). This goes well with salmon or any other fish. Marinate for up to 2 hours prior to cooking.
Prep time: 10 minutes.

Not only do marinades go great on pork and chicken, they fit seafood just as well. The whiskey marinade goes well on scallops and shrimp and even on oysters. When you shuck the oysters, pour a little of the marinade into the half shell with the oyster and then grill it. The oysters basically boil in the sauce and woooo hoooo are they good. One tip I always give in my grilling classes: grills weren't made to go on high. As a matter of fact, I don't know why they even have high settings. In all the years I have been grilling I have never cooked a thing on high. Nope, not one single thing. As a matter of fact, I've cooked on the opposite (low) more than any other setting. Keep in mind that grills cook at high temperatures, and the grates aren't all that far from the food. Even on low the flames, or coals, are at best a few inches from the food. Grilling and smoking is an experience. A journey if you will. Let it play out, cook your food on medium or low and enjoy your time with family and friends. In the end you'll be glad you did.

Holy Smokes, I'm Married

At this point in the book I'm not going to go into a dissertation on marriage. I am certainly no expert when it comes to being a great married man, even though I have spent more than a third of my life in the bonds of wedded bliss.

In a lot of ways I think of being married sort of like I do of cooking: it's a succession of ups and downs, successes and failures, problems and solutions, likes and dislikes. At the end of the day, in both marriage and in your food experiences, if the good has outweighed the bad I think you are doing pretty good.

I have been blessed in that my wife (and my entire family for that matter) has been more than receptive to my crazy concoctions, absurd ideas and remarkably wild attempts at making the perfect dish of food. She has tried most everything, be it good or bad, and very few times has she thrown up. Okay, okay I'm kidding. I can't remember a time that she (or my son) has thrown up when it could be pinpointed to the food. Circumstantial evidence may abound in some cases but there's not been a for sure gut wrenching in 15 years. In many ways that is probably what has led to my fearlessness in cooking. Oh sure, I've messed up enough food to feed a small country through the years, but boy oh boy have we eaten some fine vittles. One thing that comes right to mind is:

Easy Alfredo Sauce

So easy a Cro-Magnon man could do it!

1 quart heavy whipping cream
½ cup Parmesan cheese
2 cloves garlic chopped
Salt and pepper
1 tablespoon corn starch mixed with 8 tablespoons water
1 tablespoon olive oil

In a skillet heat one tablespoon olive oil. Add the garlic and cook for 30 seconds. Add the cream and stir constantly until it comes to a small boil. Add the Parmesan, salt and pepper and corn starch mixture. Continue stirring until sauce has thickened. Serve over chicken, noodles, or shrimp.
Prep time: 15 minutes.

Both my wife and son say that without fail this is one of the best dishes I make. It's so easy to do and will save you money over buying bottled sauce, not to mention you don't have to stomach all the things that go into bottled sauces. You can serve that sauce plain over noodles or you can add some grilled chicken, fish or shrimp. In a separate skillet add some olive oil, a pinch of dried basil and 2 chicken breasts (or 2 tilapia fillets or 1 pound of medium shrimp) cut into ½" slices. Cook until the meat is no longer pink and place over the noodles. Top with the sauce. The one comment I get more than any is, "Surely it can't be that easy!" Yes it can, and stop calling me Shirley. To make one of the most spectacular recipes any human being can whip up, make the sauce and use it in:

White Lasagna
My wife's all-time favorite recipe.

2 cups Easy Alfredo Sauce (see recipe) or 1 large jar Alfredo Sauce
2 packages frozen chopped spinach, drained and patted dry
1 cup cottage cheese
1 cup ricotta cheese
1 lb. ground chicken or turkey
1 lb. Italian sausage
1 cup sliced black olives
1 cup sliced mushrooms
1 large onion, chopped
1 package shredded romano cheese
2 packages shredded mozzarella cheese
1 cup Parmesan cheese
9 lasagna noodles, cooked

Brown the ground chicken and Italian sausage in a skillet with the onions. Drain and mix with the Alfredo sauce in a large bowl. Spray a 13x9 pan with non-stick spray. Begin by putting a thin layer of the meat mixture on the bottom of the pan, cover with 3 noodles, then a layer of cottage cheese and ricotta cheese (these can be combined into one layer), a layer of spinach, olives, mushrooms and mozzarella. Continue with layers ending with a meat layer on top. Place a layer of mozzarella cheese on top and sprinkle with the Parmesan. Bake at 375 degrees for 45 minutes or until heated throughout. This recipe can be made up prior to cooking and refrigerated or frozen until ready to cook. Be sure to fully thaw if frozen and increase cooking time to 1 hour.
Prep time: 30 minutes. Servings: 8.

To take this recipe a little further add some cooked, chopped bacon to the sauce. You now have a carbonara sauce that's out of this world good. I know it's hard to believe but we just made an awesome Italian dish and didn't break the bank or spend two days doing it. There are many great things about being married of course, but one thing that really sticks out is how I was able to discover the oven. Much like other people when we first got married (not unlike in this recent recession), going out to eat was a treat. As I look back on it, being a treat really wouldn't scratch the surface of what it was. I was working in construction and my wife was still in college. Money was like trying to come by a diamond. Maybe a tenth of a carat would turn up now and then, but it wasn't very often. What that means is that we spent a lot of time at home, watching television and cooking our own food. We didn't eat very extravagantly, but it was always good and there was lots of it. For instance:

Easy Meatballs

A very easy way to treat your family to homemade meatballs.
This recipe works well with ground wild game also.

1 lb. bulk Italian sausage
½ cup seasoned bread crumbs
2 eggs, lightly beaten
1 cup shredded Parmesan cheese
1 teaspoon red pepper flakes
10 oz. beer

Preheat oven to 375 degrees. Mix the Italian sausage, bread crumbs, eggs, Parmesan cheese and red pepper flakes until well combined. Roll into small meatballs, being careful not to roll too tightly. Place on an oven safe pan and bake for 25 minutes or until juices run clear. In a large pot bring the beer to a boil. Add the meatballs and cook for 3 minutes. Remove meatballs, add sauce of your choice and serve over pasta.
Prep time: 20 minutes. Servings: 4.

These meatballs can be made with basically any kind of ground meat so you can really save some money if you buy ground meat in bulk. Keep your eyes open for specials on ground meat at your local grocery, as they often run deals on these items. They are very easy to make and don't take a lot of time, leaving you free to do other things around the house, like catch up on football scores… not that I would know. They can be served with canned spaghetti sauce and noodles, with the Easy Alfredo sauce we made earlier or even put into a crock pot with grape jelly and chili sauce as an appetizer. Another great dish that I really started making in the early days of our marriage which also happens to be another of my wife's favorites is:

Cheesy Chicken
We made this recipe weekly the first year we were married.

4 large chicken breasts sliced into ¼" thick slices
1 cup salsa
4 cheese slices
Salt and pepper
1 can cream of broccoli soup
Hot cooked rice
Sour cream
1 tablespoon olive oil

Put chicken in a skillet with 1 tablespoon of olive oil. Sauté until no longer pink. Add the cream of broccoli soup and the salt and pepper. Stir until heated throughout. Remove several slices of chicken from skillet and place on a bed of hot rice. Top with a cheese slice and a tablespoon of salsa. Add a tablespoon of sour cream if desired.
Prep time: 20 minutes. Servings: 4.

Looking back, I think we lived on that chicken recipe for a good while. Every time I turned around the wife was requesting it and to be honest, when Momma asks for something usually she gets it. After all, if Momma ain't happy, Daddy surely ain't happy. Oddly enough, in those early days of our marriage I didn't fry much. I kept it simple, made things that I thought we would both like and hoped for the best. If marriage has taught me anything about cooking it's that you must always think of your spouse first when it comes to food. I have had a lot of trials and tribulations in the kitchen, but nothing hurts worse than spending hours making something, investing your heart and soul into a dish, only to find it gets a lukewarm reception. Again, my family has rarely said that something stinks, but sometimes it doesn't take words to know what they are feeling. The tip that I give in my cooking classes early and often is to not get too emotionally attached to your creations. It does sound corny, but it's hard not to feel extra special about something that you may have put several hours into making. Expect it to be good, but don't fret if it gets a less than expected reaction. People's taste buds are as unique as their fingerprints. I like to say, you never truly know someone until you've cooked for them. Speaking of cooking, I used to put this recipe together on weekends, or when we had company coming over:

Lasagna
This is one of my son's all-time favorites.

1 large jar spaghetti sauce
1 small container cottage cheese
1 package pepperoni
1 lb. ground beef
1 package Italian sausage
2 small cans sliced black olives
1 small can sliced green olives
2 small cans sliced mushrooms
1 large onion, chopped
2 packages shredded mozzarella cheese
½ cup Parmesan cheese
9 lasagna noodles, cooked

Brown the ground beef and Italian sausage in a skillet with the onions. Drain and mix with the jar of spaghetti sauce in a large bowl. Spray a 13x9 pan with non-stick spray. Begin by putting a thin layer of the meat mixture on the bottom of the pan, cover with 3 noodles, a layer of cottage cheese, a layer of pepperoni, olives, mushrooms and mozzarella. Continue with layers ending with a meat layer on top. Put a layer of cheese on top and sprinkle with the Parmesan. Bake at 375 for 45 minutes or until heated throughout. This recipe can be made up prior to cooking and refrigerated or frozen until ready to cook. Be sure to fully thaw if frozen and increase cooking time to 1 hour.
Prep time: 30 minutes. Servings: 8.

Lasagna is great in so many ways. It makes a bunch, so there are usually leftovers, and most importantly it's liked by almost everyone. I'm not saying that every human being on earth loves lasagna, but you can be pretty safe in assuming that if people eat meat, they will more than likely take a spoonful of it, if nothing else to not hurt your feelings. Serve that lasagna with some garlic bread and a simple salad and you have a wonderful meal that can be made ahead of time and frozen. On a different note, it takes a good while to cook, so if your spouse is having friends over and you'd rather not hang with them you can always stay in the kitchen under the guise of making sure the lasagna doesn't burn. Never underestimate the power of food to save you from annoying friends. Another dish that's really good for entertaining is:

Chicken Enchiladas

Chicken and cheese, what a great mix!

1 large package chicken breasts
1 large onion
1 can cream of chicken soup
1 package taco seasoning
1 cup shredded cheddar cheese
1 package large tortilla shells
2 cans enchilada sauce
1 tablespoon olive oil

Cut chicken into small pieces and chop onion. Sauté in a tablespoon of olive oil until cooked through. Drain. Mix the chicken and onions, cheese, soup and taco seasoning. Spoon 2 tablespoons of chicken mixture into each tortilla. Roll the tortillas, putting them into a baking dish seam side down. Cover with enchilada sauce and bake on 325 for 45 minutes. Serve with additional cheese.
Prep time: 30 minutes. Servings 6.

I can remember back when my wife and I first got married, making those enchiladas for her cousin. She used to come and stay with us periodically. It was always great to see her and when I knew she was coming I would whip up that dish, knowing that she loved the enchiladas. Although this recipe is also one that makes it possible to hide from unwanted company, I never had to when her cousin was over. Even had I wanted to (which I didn't), I couldn't have as we lived in a trailer and the kitchen and living room were basically one small room. Notice I didn't try to convince you it was one big room. It wasn't. It was tiny. If you tripped in the living room you fell in the kitchen. When something on the stove boiled over it landed on the living room carpet. I'm not saying it was small, but the mice moved out because they were too cramped. The mouse that did stay really loved:

Pork Chops and Gravy

Serve this over noodles, cooked rice or mashed potatoes.

1 family pack pork tenderloin or pork chops
1 cup Fry Dredge
2 cans cream of mushroom soup with roasted garlic
1 medium onion, chopped
1 tablespoon seasoned salt
1 tablespoon butter
4 tablespoons milk
2 cups prepared rice
2 tablespoons olive oil

Put olive oil in a skillet over medium heat. Dredge pork and place
in skillet with chopped onions. Sauté until brown on the outside
and no longer pink on inside. Remove pork and onions from
skillet. Drain oil from skillet. Add soup, butter and milk to skillet.
Stir well. Place pork and onions on top of soup mixture. Bring to
a boil and simmer for 20. Serve over hot rice.
Prep time: 20 minutes. Servings: 4.

Actually the mouse didn't get any of it (as far as I know). I
certainly like it though, so even if the vermin didn't it was still a
big time hit. The combination of the gravy and rice really makes
for a satisfying dish, especially when its cold outside. While we are
talking about good ole stick-to-your-ribs food I just love:

Stuffed Meatloaf

A gorgeous serving when laid out in slices on a light colored dish.

5 lbs. hamburger
1 lb. thinly sliced ham (either smoked or baked)
1 lb. thinly sliced swiss cheese
3 eggs, slightly beaten
1 small onion, finely chopped
3 slices bread, crusts removed and torn into small
**   pieces**
2 cups ketchup
¼ cup A-1 steak sauce
¼ cup mustard
4 tablespoons packed brown sugar

Preheat oven to 350 degrees. In a large bowl mix the hamburger,
onion, bread and eggs together. Roll out onto a large piece of
aluminum foil that has been lightly greased. Layer the ham and
swiss cheese onto the hamburger. Beginning at a corner, roll
up the hamburger jelly roll style, being sure to seal the ends.
Place in a loaf pan. In another small bowl mix the ketchup, A-1,
mustard and brown sugar. Spoon the mixture over the meatloaf.
Place in oven and bake for 50 minutes or until cooked through.
Allow to stand for a few minutes before slicing.
Prep time: 30 minutes. Servings: 6.

I'm gonna tell you something right now, boy is that meatloaf
some fine eating. I mean really fine eating. Most times a meatloaf
is not something you think of as being exotic, but when you slice
across that and the layers of ham and cheese in the middle show up
it is really something to look at. This isn't your Mom's regular old
Sunday meatloaf. It's a true culinary delight. Be sure to have copies
of the recipe on hand as family and friends will surely ask. When it
came to making things ahead of time and then cooking them once
we were home in the evenings, the first thing that comes to mind
is:

Crab Stuffed Ham

Not just your everyday ham.

1 medium picnic ham, unsliced
1 package Stove Top Stuffing (prepared according to
 directions)
½ cup sharp cheddar cheese
1 medium sized can crabmeat, drained and picked
 through to remove shells
½ teaspoon black pepper
2 teaspoons Worcestershire sauce
1 cup brown sugar
1 cup apple cider

Preheat oven to 350 degrees. Using a sharp, thin bladed knife cut a core from the center of the ham, being careful to not go all the way through. Remove the plug and cut off the end approximately 1". Cut the rest of the ham into small pieces. Mix the stuffing, cheese, crabmeat, pepper and Worcestershire sauce and the ham pieces. Meanwhile, heat the apple cider in a medium sauce pan over medium heat. Add the brown sugar and stir to dissolve. Place as much of the stuffing into the hole in the ham as will fit, sealing with the plug. Place the ham in a large baking dish and pour over the apple cider mix. Place in oven and bake for 30 minutes or until heated throughout. Remove from oven, allow to sit for 10 minutes and slice.
Prep time: 35 minutes. Servings: 8.

Of all the recipes in this book that take a fair amount of time to prepare, this is one that really will test your patience but will be worth it in the end. It's a trial to get the center of the ham out without cutting through the other side and, more importantly, through your hand. The two best knives for work like this are a sharp ended carving or a fillet knife. Be careful not to slice through the sides as your knife works in the center. If you get a big enough ham and you have small enough hands you can loosen it with the knife and then grab it out in chunks. Also try a large fork if you have stubborn pieces. Almost like the stuffed meatloaf you really end up with a beautiful presentation with this recipe as the cross sections look fantastic on a light colored serving plate. If you aren't a crabmeat fan, use shrimp or even chopped clams in place of the crab. If you want to avoid seafood, use cooked sausage or for a vegetarian treat, add cooked peas and pearl onions. Now that I'm hungry as all get out I just remembered a recipe that I used to make, and still do, that's really easy:

Tuna Noodle Casserole

This recipe works equally well with precooked chicken.

2 large cans tuna or chicken, drained
1 can cream of mushroom soup
1 can cream of mushroom soup with roasted garlic
8 oz. shredded cheddar cheese (I use sharp cheddar)
1 can peas
½ package egg noodles, cooked
Salt and pepper

Mix all ingredients and place in a baking dish or 13x9 pan. Bake at 350 degrees for 35 to 45 minutes or until heated throughout and top is bubbly.
Prep time: 15 minutes. Servings: 8.

The garlic hint that the soup presents in this casserole really adds to the cheesiness and flair of the noodles. Again, it's a recipe that when you tell someone they automatically sigh and think, "tuna casserole, big deal." However, the minute they taste it they are typically blown away. I have served this recipe many times and have yet to not get a "WOW" somewhere along the line. It's easy, fairly quick to make and tasty. It's also excellent the following day once the flavors have married overnight. Along the same lines, another dish that really stands out to people and is just off the charts the following day:

Baked Cavatini

My go-to recipe when having company over.

1 package pepperoni
2 small cans mushrooms
2 small cans black olives
1 lb. ground beef, browned
1 large onion, chopped
1 can (12 oz.) tomato sauce
1 teaspoon Italian seasoning
½ teaspoon garlic powder (or 2 cloves fresh garlic chopped)
½ package rotini noodles (cooked) or pasta of your choice
1 package shredded Italian cheese
½ cup Parmesan cheese

Mix the tomato sauce and Italian seasoning together and set aside (it is good to have an extra can of sauce in case you like it a little wetter). Brown the ground beef and onion in a skillet and transfer to a large mixing bowl. Add the cooked noodles and other ingredients except the sauce and Italian cheese. Stir well. Add the sauce and toss to coat. Put mixture into a 13x9 pan. Cover the top with the cheeses. Bake on 350 degrees for 30 to 40 minutes or until heated throughout and cheese begins to brown on the edges.
Prep time: 20 minutes. Servings: 6.

Before you ask, cavatini is a name for a meaty dish with tomato or pasta sauce. It is, however, just a name. I like catchy names. Maybe this is catchy and maybe it's not, but I like it so it's staying. Cavatini really rolls off the tongue when you're saying it. It seems to have an air about it, almost a purpose; when you say cavatini, people are going to listen. Looking back, I see that we are really on a recipe roll right now so I'm gonna drop this little tidbit:

Pork Hotdish

Hotdish – it's not just for Northerners any more!

1 lb. pork tenderloin, cut into 1" cubes
½ lb. smoked ham, cut into ½" cubes
1 16 oz. can green beans, drained
1 green pepper, roughly chopped
1 yellow pepper, roughly chopped
1 medium onion, roughly chopped
6 tablespoons butter, divided
1 cup milk
8 oz. Velveeta cheese
8 oz. shredded cheddar cheese
½ teaspoon black pepper
½ teaspoon salt
½ teaspoon garlic powder
½ teaspoon chili powder
2 teaspoons hot sauce

Preheat oven to 400 degrees. In a large skillet heat 2
tablespoons butter over medium heat. Add the peppers and the
onion and sauté for 8 minutes or until softened. Remove from
skillet and keep warm. Add 2 tablespoons butter to skillet. Add
pork tenderloin and sauté until browned on all sides. Add ham,
salt, pepper, garlic powder, chili powder and hot sauce. Stir well
and remove from heat. Meanwhile in a large saucepan over
medium heat, add milk, remaining butter and Velveeta cheese.
Stir constantly until cheese is melted. Add cheddar and stir well.
Mix pork tenderloin with onion mixture and green beans in a
9x13 pan. Pour over cheese sauce and bake for 20 minutes.
Prep time: 20 minutes. Servings: 8.

If you are looking for a dish that simply has it all this is that
dish. Cheesy, meaty, lots of veggies. I really like it for a lot of reasons, not the least of which is it can be a real freezer-cleaner-outer.
I just coined that phrase by the way, "freezer-cleaner-outer," nice

rhyme to that. In essence, it uses up a lot of items (be they canned goods or frozen ones) that might be drawing freezer burn or sitting around in the cabinets dying of loneliness. Don't be afraid to spice that up a little more with red pepper flakes and make it a real tongue ripper. I like to eat it with crackers similar to a stew. Hotdish itself tends to be a Northern dish with few southerners having even heard the term. I have some friends who live in Wisconsin and Minnesota and they have hotdish often. I don't confess to being a snow loving Northern ice fisherman, but I do like a hotdish now and then. So, now we are all dressed up, got our Sunday best meat dishes on and no sides to go to. I guess we'd better fix that.

Sidling Up to You Babe

Like many of you reading this book, I have ups and downs in life and in cooking. One of the worst downs I have ever suffered was when I was cooking baked beans. Yep, innocent old baked beans. Who would think the common legume could lay somebody up? Truth be known, it really wasn't the beans' fault. Here's how it went down: I usually cook my baked beans in a skillet rather than putting them in a baking dish and sticking them in the oven. I guess the reason is that I like the control that I have on the stovetop better than that of the oven. Anywho, I had been whipping up a big ole batch of my almost world famous baked beans and had removed the skillet from the burner and turned it off. In a total fit of dumbness, I laid my hand on the burner without thinking about it still being hot. If you've ever seen the rings around Jupiter, that's sort of what my palm looked like. The electric rings of the burner had imprinted themselves perfectly right across my hand. I must say that of all the pain I've had in my life – broken bones, torn ligaments, girlfriends who dumped me – all of those wouldn't add up to what I was feeling right about then, made all the more painful by the realization that it wasn't even a culinary masterpiece that had injured me. It was stinking baked beans of all things. It couldn't even be a proud or elegant dish like green or Italian beans, it had to be the bottom dweller that gets relegated to being covered in bacon or fatback and put out of sight in the oven. Oh well, I healed up and this all brings me to my point here.

In my day to day cooking affairs, the one thing that I find to be the hardest is to come up with exciting, and often times new, sides. I know some of you are shaking your heads in agreement here. It's easy to say, "grilled steaks for dinner," or "how about some fried chicken, honey?" but the real challenge comes in pairing something with your entree. Even butter can only have so much of an effect on frozen vegetables. The search for outstanding sides that don't take a gargantuan effort is what led me to:

Potatoes with Butter Cream Sauce

A special holiday side dish that can be made ahead of time.

2 lbs. red potatoes or small brown potatoes
1 cup heavy cream
1 8 oz. package cream cheese, softened
1 cup sharp cheddar, shredded
¼ cup chives or green onion tops, finely chopped
1 stick butter, softened
Salt and pepper to taste

Preheat over to 400 degrees. In a large pot cover the potatoes with water and place over medium high heat. Bring to a boil and cook for 10 minutes or until tender. Remove from heat, drain and allow to sit for 10 minutes. Meanwhile, in a large saucepan over medium heat, add the cream, cream cheese and butter. Stir well until all cheese is melted. Add salt and pepper and cheddar cheese, stirring frequently until the cheese has melted. Slice the potatoes into ¼" rounds and place in a large baking dish and pour over the cream sauce. Sprinkle with the green onions. Place dish in oven and bake for 20 minutes or until hot and bubbly.
Prep time: 20 minutes. Servings: 8.

I will be the first to admit that there are some delicious recipes in this book. Heck, I'm the one eating them, so if I don't say it, who's going to? If delicious is as delicious does, then this potato recipe is one of the most delicious of the delicious. It's fantastic, and so simple to make. I recently served this recipe to my in-laws for our Christmas dinner and it was a huge hit. The cream cheese sauce makes it very elegant and the sharp cheddar gives it a nice bite. The great part is that the potatoes can be boiled ahead of time and refrigerated for a day or two, saving a lot of time when it comes to dinner day and there are fifty thousand things going on.

As with some of the others that I talked about earlier, one of the points that I really try to make in my classes and appearances is to cut down on the stress of cooking. Everything seems to taste better when you don't work yourself into a frenzy trying to get it ready, and this is especially true around the holidays. Do as much as you possibly can the days ahead of your big dinner and leave yourself more time to socialize when your family is over. I tell my son often that the best times of my life are spent with him and the rest of my family. I love cooking, but when family and friends are over it is not the time to be living in the kitchen. Another recipe that really fits the bill here is:

Mixed Vegetables
with Cajun Butter Cream Sauce

Add a sprinkle of cayenne pepper to make this spicier.

1 bag frozen mixed vegetables
1 pint heavy cream
4 tablespoons salted butter
1 teaspoon Cajun seasoning
2 teaspoon cornstarch
2 tablespoons water

Cook vegetables according to package directions. In a medium
sauce pan heat cream over medium heat. Do not boil. Add the
butter and Cajun seasoning and stir to mix. In a small bowl
mix the cornstarch and water until all lumps are gone. Slowly
add cornstarch mixture to cream, stirring well. Bring back
to temperature and stir constantly until desired thickness is
achieved. It should be like light pancake batter. Mix the cream
sauce into the vegetables and serve.
Prep time: 15 minutes. Servings: 4.

The butter cream sauce really takes the frozen vegetables to another level in this side. I love it because you can vary the vegetables
you use in it and totally change the finished product. It's quick to
make and has enough zip to impress company. Very much like:

Carrots in Horseradish Cream Sauce

My favorite way to serve carrots.

4 cups fresh carrots
½ cup heavy whipping cream
1 cup mayonnaise
3 teaspoons prepared horseradish
1 small onion, finely chopped
½ teaspoon salt
½ teaspoon fresh ground pepper
¼ cup melted butter
½ cup bread crumbs
3 cups water

Preheat oven to 350 degrees. In a large saucepan bring water to a boil. Add carrots and simmer for 8 minutes or until beginning to get tender. Remove from water and drain. In a medium sized bowl mix all the remaining ingredients except butter and bread crumbs. Add carrots and stir well. Pour into a greased 9x13 pan and place in oven. Combine butter and bread crumbs. Sprinkle over carrots. Bake for 15 minutes or until hot and bubbly. Serve immediately.
Prep time: 20 minutes. Servings: 8.

I'm not the world's biggest carrot fan, but the addition of the horseradish really makes it a knockout. I saw a similar recipe in a cookbook one time and adapted it to my tastes. All it takes is the general idea of a dish and then a little time in the kitchen to transform it into something that fits your, and your families', taste buds to the max. Another example of this is:

Rosemary and Garlic Mashed Potato Casserole

A way to take standard potato casserole to the next level.

5 lbs. potatoes, cut into ¾" pieces
2 cloves garlic, finely minced
2 sprigs fresh rosemary (see tip #19)
8 oz. sour cream
8 oz. sharp cheddar cheese
1 small onion, finely chopped
½ stick real butter
½ pint heavy cream
Salt and pepper to taste

In a large pot, boil the potatoes and rosemary until the potatoes are soft. Discard the rosemary. Drain the potatoes and place them back in the pot over the burner (this will remove any liquid that is left) for 1 minute. Remove from heat. Add the garlic, onion, sour cream, butter and cream and mash until they reach your desired consistency. Fold in the cheese and add a dash of salt and pepper. Place the potatoes in a large baking dish and bake on 350 degrees for 30 minutes or until bubbly and top has begun to brown.
Prep time: 20 minutes. Servings: 8.

This is a recipe that I adapted from a basic potato casserole that my mom makes:

Potato Casserole

Quick, easy and delicious!

2 packages prepared mashed potatoes (or 6 medium potatoes, cooked and mashed)
8 oz. sour cream
8 oz. cheddar cheese (I use sharp cheddar)

1 medium onion
2 cloves garlic (or ½ teaspoon garlic powder)
2 tablespoons butter

Chop the onion and sauté in the butter until tender (about 5 minutes). Add the garlic the last 30 seconds. Mix all ingredients in a large bowl and pour into a baking pan. Bake on 350 degrees for 35 minutes or until bubbling along the sides.
Prep time: 20 minutes. Servings: 8.

You'll see some similarities in those two recipes. Both can be made in less than an hour and both are basically the same as far as preparation, but the finished products couldn't be different. The rosemary (an herb that I love) and garlic bring a depth to this side dish that makes it extravagant. I love to serve this alongside roast or corned beef; however, it also pairs wonderfully with chicken and even fish.

A point that I want to make here: there's no book on what you have to do as far as side dishes go. So many times I hear people saying what you can and can't serve according to the meat or how it was cooked. What? Really? Someone is going to come to your house and enforce the unwritten rule that you shouldn't mix dairy and citrus? There's a food police that will arrest you if you serve two starches at the same meal? People, it's your home, its your digestive tract: do with it what you want. If you want to have mashed potatoes and corn, do it. For crying out loud, we are so caught up with what someone says we should or shouldn't do with our sides that we forget what's most important, our own taste buds.

I can't tell you how many times I've laughed when hearing people talk about the "dos and don'ts" of cooking. I'm going to let you in on something that has taken me years, and I mean years, to learn. Maybe even decades to learn. Maybe even millennium, although that sounds a bit long for this insight. Here it goes, the most important cooking information ever: the only thing you "can't" do in cooking is what you aren't willing to try. That's pretty deep I realize, but it's true. If you want to do it, then by all means do so. If it's good, tell your friends; if it stinks, don't tell anyone. Now back to where we were before I went off on my tangent. Another recipe that really exemplifies what I am talking about is:

Wilted Lettuce
The number one reason I plant lettuce in my garden.

1 large head bibb or garden fresh lettuce (not iceberg), torn into medium size pieces
5 strips bacon
½ cup water
¼ cup cider vinegar
3 tablespoons sugar
1 teaspoon black pepper

In a large skillet, fry bacon until crispy. Remove bacon but leave drippings in pan. In a small bowl mix the water, vinegar, sugar and pepper. Add to the skillet, being careful to not splash out the bacon drippings. Heat to boiling and simmer for 1 minute. Crumble bacon. Put lettuce in a large serving bowl and pour over the vinegar dressing. Sprinkle with bacon. Serve immediately. Prep time: 10 minutes. Servings: 4.

I am a real fan of this recipe. It's best when made using fresh garden lettuce, but tastes almost as good with store-bought leaf lettuce. Iceberg is too tough and tends to curl up if used in this recipe, so try to stick with one of the great, and very available, leaf lettuces that are available in most grocery stores. Simplicity is the real key here, but don't get ahead of yourself on making it. This recipe doesn't stand up well and should be made just before serving. Along the same lines as this recipe comes this one which is my son's all-time favorite side dish:

Easy Greens
My son will eat the entire pot of these greens by himself.

10 cups fresh turnip or collard greens (the bagged ones work great)
1 medium onion
3 cups water
1 link Polish sausage
2 tablespoons olive oil
2 tablespoons apple cider vinegar

Chop the onion and cut the sausage into small pieces. Put all ingredients in a large pot and cover. Bring to a boil, lower temp and simmer for 45 minutes. Season with salt and pepper. Drain and serve.
Prep time: 10 minutes. Servings: 4.

As recipes in this book, and most other cookbooks for that matter go, this is one of the easiest and most straight forward you will ever try. As I said, its one of my son's favorite foods and by far his favorite sides. If it takes a little sausage or vinegar to get him to eat greens, I am going to do it. One of the big challenges in cooking is getting people to not only eat but to enjoy what you are cooking. This is especially true of children. Kids are funny like that sometimes. They will love something one day, and want so much you think they will explode, and the next time they won't even try a bite of it. My wife and I have been very fortunate in that our son will try and eat most anything. However, I know tons of people who can't get their children to eat anything other than chicken strips and french fries. Now, I don't claim to be a guru of getting your little curtain climbers to eat exotic food, but I will say that the best chance for success lies in making things that they like some portion of. By that I mean, if your kids like cheese, try putting cheese with their vegetables. I have put cheese in peas, carrots, broccoli and more, but one of the best things I have cheesed up is:

Ultimate 4-Cheese Baked Macaroni

Not your average mac and cheese!

1 box macaroni or rotini pasta
½ stick real butter
3 tablespoons bread crumbs
2 cups milk
1 cup shredded sharp cheddar cheese
1 cup shredded (or grated) Romano cheese
1 cup shredded Swiss cheese
1 cup shredded Monterrey jack cheese, divided
3 tablespoons flour
Fresh grated salt and pepper

Preheat oven to 375 degrees. In a small sauce pan, warm milk but do not boil. Meanwhile in a large high sided skillet melt the butter over medium heat. Add the warmed milk a little at a time and stir well. Add the flour and stir so that all lumps are broken up. Stir constantly for 8 to 10 minutes or until thick and well incorporated. Add all the cheeses except the reserved half of the Monterrey Jack, along with the salt and pepper and stir until cheeses are melted. Set aside. In a large pot boil the macaroni for 3 minutes. It will not be tender. Drain and spray lightly with cool water. Drain once again. Add the macaroni to the skillet with the cheese sauce and stir to incorporate. Pour into a large baking dish, cover with remaining cheese and bread crumbs and place in the preheated oven for 30 minutes (or until well browned on top). Remove from oven and allow standing for a few minutes. Prep time: 30 minutes. Servings: 8.

The recipes in this book tend to be fairly easy to make. For the most part that is simply because it's my belief if you make things hard, they tend not to get accomplished. This macaroni recipe is one of the harder ones in this book, although it's by no means too difficult for anyone to attempt. Without a doubt, this is my wife's favorite side dish, which just goes to show how much of a family man I really am. Heck, I have listed both my son's and my wife's favorite sides and have not listed my own yet. Gosh, I'm such a touchy-feely guy. Speaking of being touchy-feely, one of the recipes that this brings to mind is:

Tomato Insalata with Balsamic Reduction
So quick and easy to make, it can be done at a moment's notice.

5 medium tomatoes, sliced and cores removed
6 oz. fresh mozzarella cheese, sliced into ¼" slices
20 fresh basil leaves
¾ cup Balsamic Reduction (see recipe below)
Salt and pepper to taste

Slice a thin piece off the bottom of the tomatoes so they sit flat. Layer the tomatoes, cheese and basil leaves, finishing with a tomato slice on top. Sprinkle with salt and pepper. Drizzle with the Balsamic Reduction and serve immediately.
Prep time: 10 minutes. Servings: 5.

Balsamic Reduction
A skillet and some balsamic vinegar, that's all you need.

1½ cups good quality balsamic vinegar

Heat a skillet over medium heat. Add the balsamic vinegar and stir constantly. Simmer until vinegar has reduced by half and has thickened slightly.
Prep time: 2 minutes.

You are probably thinking to yourself, why would tomatoes and vinegar make me think of being touchy-feely? It makes me think of touchy-feely because it takes some handling to put it together. I must confess that I like recipes that you get your hands dirty making. I like feeling like my hands have created something and that the finished product is a result of how you are as a food craftsman. This tomato recipe fits the bill perfectly and it's super fast and easy to put together. You can assemble the tomato and mozzarella stacks ahead of time and simply make your reduction and drizzle it over the stacks just before serving. The reduction will take around 10 minutes, according to how much of it you are making and how hot your skillet is when you add the vinegar. This is a great recipe to let the kids help with. Slice the tomatoes and cheese and let the kids put the stacks together. They will enjoy putting the stacks together and hopefully they will take to eating them since they have a vested interest in the creation. Another recipe that tends to be a little harder than some but that is more than worth the time is:

Chicken Garlic Salsa Deviled Eggs

They take a little time, but the result is more than worth the trouble.

18 eggs, hardboiled and split in half
4 cloves roasted garlic
3 tablespoons cooked chicken breast, shredded
3 tablespoons Garlic salsa (see recipe below)
1 tablespoon sour cream
1 teaspoon apple cider vinegar
1 teaspoon mayonnaise
1 teaspoon paprika
1 teaspoon Parmesan cheese

Remove the yolks from the eggs and place in a large bowl. Smash the yolks with a fork. Add the remaining ingredients except the paprika and Parmesan. Fold the ingredients together and spoon or pipe into the egg whites. Sprinkle the eggs with the paprika and Parmesan.
Prep time: 20 minutes. Servings: 6.

Garlic Salsa

Great served as a side with chips and sour cream.

6 Roma tomatoes, chopped
4 tablespoons red onion, chopped
4 cloves garlic, chopped
1 can diced tomatoes with green chilies
1 can chopped tomatoes with garlic and onions
1 teaspoon dried mustard
1 teaspoon cumin
½ cup oil and vinegar
¼ cup cilantro, finely chopped

Add all ingredients to a large non-reactive bowl (see tip #20).
Mix well with a spoon and allow to sit for 1 hour.
Prep time: 15 minutes.

You may not have guessed it, although that would be hard not to do, but I love eggs. I really love eggs. I love fried eggs, poached eggs, boiled eggs and scrambled eggs but at the top of my list is deviled. I'll drop another recipe on you in just a minute that is my go to recipe for deviled eggs. When I have some extra time I love to whip up these extra special deviled delights. The garlic finish that these eggs present is unlike any other deviled egg you will ever try. They make a fabulous side dish, but I like to eat them as snacks. They tend not to last very long around our house.

One thing to keep in mind here is that eggs, specifically deviled eggs, more specifically garlic deviled eggs, can really have an effect on the gastronomic system of some people. Basically in a nut shell, don't serve these on a first date with someone you might want to keep around for a while. They can be a real relationship killer; if she, or he, can stand to be around you an hour after eating them, they might just be a keeper. You probably have real marriage material on your hands right there, so that's another reason to be careful. The last thing you need is to hook someone on garlic deviled eggs when you might not be serious about them. That's about like letting a vampire bite you if you aren't sure you want to live forever. Not very good planning I would say. In any case, they are certainly special and take the regular old deviled treat to a new high.

I promised earlier that I would divulge one of my most tightly guarded recipes, that being my everyday deviled eggs so here goes:

Mexican Deviled Eggs
My everyday deviled egg recipe.

12 eggs, boiled and cut in half, yolks removed to a bowl
¼ cup sour cream
3 tablespoons salsa
2 tablespoons mayo
1 tablespoon olive oil
1 tablespoon cider vinegar
2 tablespoons Parmesan cheese
Salt and pepper to taste
Smoked paprika to sprinkle

Crumble the yolks and add all the other ingredients except the smoked paprika. Put the filling in a Ziploc bag and cut one corner of the bag off. Pipe the filling into the eggs and sprinkle with the smoked paprika.
Prep time: 20 minutes. Servings: 6.

Even I find it odd that being an old boy from the hills of Kentucky my "hole card" deviled eggs are Mexican. Actually, I only call them that because of the salsa, not because I have any Spanish blood coursing through my veins. Actually I have told my wife that as much as I love Mexican food I might very well be 100% Mexican. However, according to my family tree that's not the case. I suspect there's a government conspiracy that's hiding my true identity from me, for reasons known only to people high up in clandestine operations. In any case, I love these deviled eggs and they are probably unlike anything else you have tried. Most deviled eggs tend to be sweet, due to sweet relish being a main ingredient. They tend to have a thicker consistency to the centers than what this recipe does. These Mexican Deviled Eggs are very easy to make. What I like to do is make the filling, put it in a Ziploc bag and refrigerate it, then just before serving clip off a corner of the bag and pipe the filling into the hollowed out eggs. There's very little waste this way and they look really nice piped rather than dropped in by spoonfuls. There are several really nice deviled egg platters available today that have a refrigerated insert to keep the eggs cool. It's great for cookouts and other outdoor gatherings in weather that's too warm for them to set out unprotected. Keep the hollowed out eggs in the tray and the filling in a cooler. Simply open the platter and pipe just before eating. All this talk about eggs and deviling them has got me to thinking about:

Roasted Mushrooms with Garlic and Herbs

Super flavor without a ton of work.

3 cups white mushrooms (button mushrooms), cut in half
3 cloves garlic, finely chopped
3 tablespoons olive oil
3 tablespoons dry white wine
4 tablespoons tomato paste
1 teaspoon fresh thyme, finely chopped
½ teaspoon fresh oregano, finely chopped

Heat a large skillet over medium heat. Add olive oil and garlic and sauté for 1 minute. Add the mushrooms, wine and tomato paste and stir well. Add the thyme and oregano and cook for 10-15 minutes or until most of the liquid is evaporated. Remove to a serving bowl.
Prep time: 15 minutes. Servings: 4.

You might be wondering why I would think of roasted mushrooms when I had been immersed in a deluge of deviled decadence.

Well, there's really no good reason for that other than the fact that I love food, and throughout the day I am going to be thinking of it in one fashion or another. I can't tell you how many times I have been sitting in a restaurant having a nice lunch, stuffed like a tick on a hound dog and all the while I am planning where and what I am going to have for supper. It's just what my DNA is made of, or maybe who my DNA is, according to how you look at it. My DNA is mostly food based. There's really no ladder shape to it. It's mostly shaped like donuts or in some cases a platter with high sides and steeped full of cheesy goodness.

So roasted mushrooms, huh. Yes, and boy are they tasty. The wine really adds a nice sparkle to them and the herbs balance out the natural flavor and chewy consistency of the 'shrooms. Like many other recipes herein, the ingredients are very easy to come by and if you have an herb garden you can substitute other fresh herbs you might have on hand. Try some sage in place of the thyme for a great, meaty flavor, or toss in a little minced up rosemary (not too much rosemary or you will overpower the dish) for an earthy goodness that really exemplifies what mushrooms are all about. Mushrooms tend to be easy to cook last minute as well because they don't require a lot of time from package to plate. They don't last real long in the refrigerator so use them quickly and replace often. Wine doesn't last too long either but as I said before that's a subject for another book. Not really along the lines of mushrooms, but certainly delicious none-the-less is:

Orzo Pasta with Black Beans and Olive Oil

Orzo pasta should be in your pantry.
It's quick, easy, and makes a great side dish.

1 lb. orzo pasta, cooked according to package
2 medium tomatoes, chopped
1 can black beans, drained and rinsed
1 jalapeno, seeded and finely chopped

1 red pepper, chopped
3 garlic cloves, finely chopped
1 sweet onion, chopped
½ cup olive oil
Salt and pepper to taste

In a small skillet add the jalapeno and red pepper and sauté for
5 minutes over medium heat. Add the garlic and turn the heat
off. Allow the oil to sit for 5 minutes. Meanwhile combine the orzo,
beans, tomatoes and onion in a large bowl. Pour in the oil and
peppers and stir to mix. Season with salt and pepper. Refrigerate
for 1 hour to overnight for flavors to marry.
Prep time: 20 minutes. Servings: 6.

Pasta, now there's a food we can all sink our teeth into, especially when it's paired with good olive oil and black beans. This
dish is one of the most beautiful recipes you can serve to guests
with the red pepper, green from the jalapeno and black from the
beans offsetting the pasta and onions. If you have a white or light
colored serving dish use it to present this and wow the crowd,
whether its friends or just you and the significant other. This recipe
is very good served warm or cold. If you are pressed for time, or
are making a huge dinner that comes with the pressure spigot in
your brain turned to high, make it the day before and keep it in the
refrigerator. Simply set it out an hour or so ahead of time and let
it come to room temperature and it will be extra special. In some
ways it's like a soup that gets better if it has a chance to sit and let
the flavors marry somewhat before serving. Now that we've hit on
black beans, let's do a little exploring south of Kentucky, like several hundred miles south.

Aaaaeeeeiiii!

That's right, Ladies and Gentlemen, children of all ages, it's time to get going on the down south side of cooking. I'm sure the majority of you have heard a good aaaaeeeeiiii in your day, but that's one of the best right there. That my friends is my, "let's get it on (culinarily speaking), war whoop." If you are ever around me and I let out one of those roars, grab a fork, cause it's getting ready to be on big time! After reading some of the recipes and stories in this book, you know that I am a spicy sort of fellow. Spicy in many ways actually, but spicy food is the one I am going to focus on here. Having eaten just about every cuisine on the planet, I can say with a straight face that I pretty much love them all, however like most people, I do have favorites. Mostly it's certain types or styles of cooking and cuisine that I like a little bit more than others. At the very top of my list, .00000001 ahead of the next type on the list, is Mexican food.

I spoke a little earlier about how much I love Mexican food, and boy I wasn't kidding. I really, really love Mexican food. I guess the real reason why people like certain foods, other than the fact that their genes are wired for liking it, is the fact that they like the ingredients. To a lesser extent, the preparation methods of that specific food style are a factor in like and dislike as well. For instance, I love peppers. Red, green, jalapeno, banana, it doesn't matter. I love them all. A lot of Mexican food is predicated on the use of peppers. Therefore, I probably would be wired internally to like it. The same goes with tomatoes, tortillas, black beans and so on and so forth. In essence, what I am saying is that the sum of the parts equals the whole. In addition to the food, I love the techniques used for Mexican cuisine.

In one of my cooking classes a while back I had the privilege of having a lady from a local Mexican restaurant and her assistant as guest speakers. I don't know that "speakers" is the correct term to use, as they were very soft-spoken and I did most of the talking, while they showed me their techniques for making the fabulous dishes that we sampled that evening. Not only did they use techniques and ingredients that just about anyone can get their hands on, even on short notice, they also can teach us tons about using all of what we cook. They are great stewards of food. What I mean by that is they utilize things that most people would never think of using. For instance, when they cook chicken it's usually boiled (at least in the recipes that they cooked in the class) and the water is then used for cooking rice and so on. I am aware that many people native to this country make stock using chicken, but not to nearly the extent of using all things like they did in the class. It's magnificent to watch them go about their cooking, a little of this, a little of that and then WHAM there's a dish bursting with flavors and colors sitting right in front of you, pervading your nostrils with aromatic goodness. What those wonderful smells and tastes mainly come from is the use of peppers, herbs and other fresh ingredients. There has certainly been a big growth of herb gardening in this country over the past decade. We are just now realizing how easy they are to utilize in our everyday cooking, and what a difference they can make to our taste buds.

Growing up, I cannot remember anyone around who had an herb garden. The only herbs around were the one's that would get you arrested if you were caught growing them. That being the case, it's easy to see why we have been slow to pick up on the use of those same ingredients in our cooking. If you grow up making lasagna with bottled sauce the idea of making your own is foreign to you, and the same goes for incorporating herbs in your foods. In a lot of ways it's like having a vegetable garden. If you didn't grow up with one, more than likely you won't just decide to plant one unless your psychologist suggests it. I am happy that my son appreciates that fresh herbs are becoming more common. He is already familiar with cutting our herbs, mincing them and their use in our sauces and casseroles. I love the fact that he can go to the grocery today and browse through an isle that has hundreds of Mexican foods. Heck, when I was a kid the closest thing to Mexican food in the grocery was bottled salsa, and that was made in New York City. I can't remember my grandma ever handling an avocado much less cooking with one. The influx of Mexican culture has really served to bring us a new attitude toward our foods and I for one love it. Probably my favorite Mexican food is one of the easiest to prepare.

Guacamole

The main reason I try to always keep tortilla chips around.

4 avocados (try to pick ones that are beginning to turn black but are still firm)
2 cloves garlic
Juice from one lime
¼ cup red onion, finely chopped
3 Roma tomatoes, chopped

Slice the avocados in half and scoop out the flesh with a spoon. Smash the flesh with a couple of forks until it's fairly smooth. Add the other ingredients and mix well. Refrigerate for an hour, or up to overnight. Stir before serving.
Prep time: 20 minutes.

The great thing here is that it really is that easy to make. It's simple. After a few times you could make it in your sleep, although I wouldn't suggest having white sheets on the bed when you did. If you're feeling froggy, chop up a jalapeno and throw in there for good measure. In a lot of ways I think this recipe exemplifies what Mexican food is all about, which is simple preparation and lots of flavor. Another dish that I truly adore is:

Chilaquiles

Pronounced chill-aa-key-lays.

2 cups shredded chicken
2 cups tortilla chips or fried tortillas, broken into
  pieces
1 cup Chilaquiles sauce (see recipe below)
2 cups melted white queso or Monterrey jack cheese

Place the tortilla chips on a large platter, pour over the sauce
and wait a couple of minutes for the chips to soak it up. Sprinkle
the chicken over and cover with the melted cheese.
Prep time: 15 minutes. Servings: 6.

Chilaquiles Sauce

Use this versatile sauce on tacos and as a chip dip.

2 lbs. Roma tomatoes
4 jalapenos
8 cups water

In a large pot bring the water to a boil. Add the tomatoes and
jalapenos and return to a boil. Continue to boil for 4 minutes or
until peppers and tomatoes are soft. Drain the water, reserving
a cup of the liquid. In small batches process the tomatoes and
peppers until a lumpy sauce forms, adding reserved liquid as
needed to make the sauce smoother. Refrigerate any unused
sauce or freeze for later use.
Prep time: 15 minutes.

Boy, was that easy and it sure is tasty. The ladies were kind
enough to make that recipe for us in the class and now I try to
order it every time I go to their restaurant. Most times Maria won't
let me though, as she knows I need to be eating different things

every time I go. In some ways I think she has taken on the task of educating me on all of great foods and traditions of Mexican cooking. When it comes to cooking or eating I tend to be a very good student so her task is not a daunting one. What all this underscores is that no matter how much kitchen experience you have as long as you have a stove, a large pot and some water you can cook Mexican food. Almost as simple as Chilaquiles is:

Tortilla Soup
Brothy goodness; great when the weather isn't so.

6 cups chicken or garlic broth
3 tablespoon olive oil, plus 2 tablespoons
1 small onion, roughly chopped
1 garlic clove, minced
2 15 oz. cans diced tomatoes
1 tablespoon tomato paste
12 tortillas, cut into strips
4 tablespoons cilantro
1 cup shredded chicken (optional)

In a large pot sauté the onion in 3 tablespoons of oil for 5 minutes or until it is tender. Add the garlic and cook for 1 minute. Add the tomatoes and tomato paste. Cook for 5 minutes and add broth. Bring to a low simmer and cook for 30 minutes. In a large skillet (or on a baking pan in the oven) crisp the tortilla strips by frying in 2 tablespoons of oil (or cooking in a 350 degree oven until crisp). Drain the strips on paper towels. Once the soup has cooked for 30 minutes add the chicken (if using) and the tortilla strips to the soup. Add the cilantro and stir well. Serve immediately.
Prep Time: 30 minutes. Servings: 10.

Once again we see an awesome tasting recipe that takes very little time and effort. The cilantro really makes this recipe as it does in many Mexican dishes, which just goes to show how powerful a small bit of fresh herbs can be. On a quick side note, herbs are one of the easiest plant groups you can grow. I have literally scattered cilantro on the ground and had a great crop of it come up. Herbs tend to take well to planters and even if you don't have much space you can still grow them successfully as long as you water them regularly and keep them in a sunny spot.

Now back to the recipe: don't add the tortilla strips more than fifteen minutes before you are going to serve the soup, as they will get squishy in no time at all. One thing that I like to do is put the tortilla strips in bowls along with shredded cheese, sour cream and salsa and let people serve themselves. A bowl of chopped cilantro will allow people to add more should they be big-time cilantro fans. For a change, replacing the diced tomatoes with Ro-Tel or fire roasted tomatoes can bring a new depth to the soup without adding additional work.

To make garlic broth, simply boil two heads of garlic, yep two heads and not two cloves, that you have cut the tops off of in a gallon of water for 1 hour. Strain out the cloves and freeze if you want to keep it or refrigerate if you are going to use it within a couple of days. For added flavor throw in a few sage leaves and a few sprigs of rosemary. Straining those off with the cloves and discarding them will leave a delicious broth that not only goes well in this tortilla soup but in many other dishes as well. I hope Maria doesn't kill me for this, but you are going to flip over this recipe:

Spanish Rice

I could eat my weight in this easy-to-prepare side dish.

1 cup long-grain or brown rice
2½ cups chicken stock
1 tomato bouillon cube (available at Mexican groceries)
½ cup canola oil

Place the oil in a medium sauce pan over medium heat. Add the rice and sauté for 5 minutes, stirring occasionally. Add the bouillon cube and mash with a fork to incorporate. Stir well and sauté for 2 minutes. Add the stock, cover and cook for 45 minutes or until liquid has absorbed and rice is tender.
Prep time: 15 minutes. Servings: 6.

If you have ever been in a Mexican restaurant and loved the rice they serve, you are not alone. I stand proudly alongside you, as do many other people. Lift those heads people, smile at the on-coming sun, feel the beating in your chest that reminds you that life is truly wonderful and Mexican rice is really that good.

Alright, I know that was a little over the top, but that's the point I am trying to make here. You can do that. In your home. With your pots and pans. I am serious about this. Half of the battle is simply believing that you really can do it. I can't tell you how many people have told me, "I don't have the pots to make that," or "I don't have the time." Not only can it be done, it can be done easily. So many people talk themselves out of doing something long before they have ever attempted to do it in the first place. I am guilty of having done that myself in the past. It's much easier to sit back and convince yourself that you can't do it then it is to actually try it the first time. Look at all the great things that we don't have in our lives because no one has taken the time to invent them. I can't really think of any of them because they are not invented yet, but I am certain that these things will exist in the future and that we are missing out on them right now. I am not going to let that happen and here is proof:

Mexican Salad

Great for potlucks, this recipe makes a lot
and the dressing will hold up to warm temps.

4 cups fresh spinach
½ cup black olives, drained
1 can black beans, drained and rinsed
1 red pepper, thinly sliced
1 red onion, thinly sliced
4 hard boiled eggs, sliced
4 slices bacon, fried crisp and broken up
¾ cup Italian dressing
½ cup mild salsa
½ teaspoon garlic powder
½ teaspoon black pepper
½ teaspoon cumin
Salt and pepper to taste

Mix the dressing, salsa, garlic powder, black pepper and cumin in a small bowl. Mix all the salad ingredients in a large bowl placing the egg slices on last. Sprinkle with salt and pepper. Add dressing and toss just before serving.
Prep time: 20 minutes. Servings: 10.

Very few recipes get any easier than that one. I would put more "verys" in front of that but it probably wouldn't make any difference. It's so easy and when you serve it people will ask you where your sombrero is. It's that good. The addition of black beans and black olives give it a texture that you find with very few salad ingredients, while the red onion and red pepper allow it to stand out on the plate. The cumin really rocks the dressing to another level. If you want it to rock the taste buds even more, use spicy salsa or even green salsa and the flavor will be off the charts. There are not a lot of times that a salad will get you this many comments but this one is a crowd pleaser. I have sent this with my wife to her company functions and the bowl always comes back empty along with multiple requests for the recipe. If you're not a spinach fan, replace it with leaf lettuce or bibb lettuce. I wouldn't recommend iceberg. I usually don't recommend iceberg unless you are making lettuce wraps, so that's not too unusual for me. Now that we've delved into some south of the border goodies, it's time to keep it down south where the weather's always warm and the coffee always has chicory.

A Little Bit More

Lagnaippe, pronounced lan-yap. "What the heck is that?" you may be wondering. "Has this boy been in the coffee and Bailey's again?" Well the answer is no. Actually the answer is yes, but it means no. I have been in the coffee and Bailey's, but not in excess. I don't drink in excess any longer. Too many memories of headaches and sour stomachs for me to go there any more. Lagnaippe, meaning to get a little more, is a common practice in Louisiana still to this day. As a side note, my favorite restaurant in Destin, Florida still uses this in their name as well.

Lagnaippe means what it says, which is basically to get a little more. A baker's dozen, for instance, when you ordered a dozen or someone throwing you in a few extra sprigs of cilantro if you bought some, that sort of thing. We used to see that sort of thing around here as well, but it slowly went by the wayside. Having been to my adopted home city of New Orleans on many occasions, I can honestly say if you are a true foodie, it's paradise. Without a doubt there are people reading this that are shaking their heads, but folks I am telling you it's worth going simply for the food. Does it have rough areas, places you shouldn't go? Absolutely. So does every other major city in the country and in the world for that matter. The thing that makes New Orleans, and Louisiana as a whole for that matter, different is the eclectic mix of food and fun that you will find around every street corner. Food, music, shopping, it's all there and I LOVE IT! I love to walk the streets, listen to the music, pop in a restaurant and have a snack, muffaletta sandwich or beignet and move on to the next place. A person can literally eat all day long and not eat at the same place twice. One of my favorite Cajun dishes to make is:

Red Beans 'n Rice
The roux makes this dish extra hearty.

1 lb. andouille sausage, cut into ½" pieces
2 cans dark red kidney beans
4 tablespoons bacon fat
4 tablespoons all purpose flour
1 small onion, finely chopped
1 small red pepper, finely chopped
1 cup brown rice (not Minute Rice)
2 cups chicken stock
½ teaspoon Cajun seasoning
2 bay leaves

Melt the bacon fat in a large pot and add flour. Stir constantly over medium heat until a medium brown roux is formed (see passage below about roux). Add the onions and pepper, cover and simmer for 5 minutes. Add the sausage and continue to simmer for 5 minutes more. Add all remaining ingredients and cover. Simmer for 35-45 minutes, stirring occasionally until the rice is tender. It may be necessary to add more stock as time goes if it is getting too thick; however, don't add too much stock without giving it a bit of time as the vegetables will render liquid into the dish as they soften. Remove bay leaves and serve.
Prep time: 30 minutes. Servings: 8.

By the way, andouille is pronounced an-do-wee and is available in most grocery stores around the country. I actually saw andouille on a shelf in a grocery store in Anchorage, Alaska, which shows its popularity. Andouille is a pork sausage typically flavored with pepper, onions and other goodies. It comes in links but occasionally you can find it in bulk, which I really like to use in soups. Andouille is very popular in Cajun cooking, but if you are pressed or can't find it, use regular smoked sausage in its place.

Before I go any further, I should spend a few minutes and a few lines talking about roux. Roux is to Cajun cooking as wheels are to a vehicle. It's that important. It is the wing of an aircraft, the roof of a house and the sand in concrete. If you mess up the roux the entire dish will suffer. If a roux is ever ruined you can't salvage it. You dump it, clean the pot and start anew. So what is roux? **Roux** is a mix of oil and flour that is cooked to the desired color and used to add flavor and thickening to a dish. Are you simply cooking flour in oil? Well, in some ways yes you are; however, some dishes call for making roux using butter in place of oil. Step by step, here it is.

To make roux you place a medium size saucepan on medium heat. Add your oil and your flour and begin stirring until it is well incorporated. The key to roux, and I mean the absolute key, is to stir constantly. In case someone missed that, I am going to say it again, stirring constantly is the key. My son makes a wonderful roux, but about halfway through he hates the stirring and wants to quit. It's a tedious process at times, especially if you want it to take it to a dark stage for duck or other wild game. It's worth it in the end, as you will see. So, you've got the flour and oil in the pan and it's basically the consistency of thin pancake batter. The first stage you will come to is blond. **Blond roux** is just beginning to darken and it's a sandy tan color. If you are using delicate ingredients or you don't want the finished product to have a dark color, now is the time to start adding your other ingredients. If you are using duck, goose, venison or other dark meats you can keep right on cooking it. The next stage you will come to is **brown roux**. One thing to keep in mind here is that for the most part these are the names that I have given this. I haven't searched it myself, but there may not be a Google page under the title brown roux. By this point your flour is really cooking and the color is what I call true brown, basically a nice medium brown. One thing to keep in mind here, the longer you cook the flour the less liquid it will absorb. What this means is if you want a really thick consistency in your finished product you will have to make more dark roux than you would light roux, simply because the dark doesn't have the ability to absorb liquid as well. If you wanted a dark roux, you kept on cooking and stirring until it reached the last stage before being burned, which is **dark roux**. It will be a real chocolate brown and be very aromatic. During this process if you see any black flecks or it starts to smell burned you need to immediately remove it from the burner and stir very well. If the flecks don't disappear you need to dump it and start all over. If your roux takes on a burned taste the entire dish will reflect this. You are better off starting over and using a little more flour and oil rather than throwing away a pound of sausage and all the other ingredients. Once you have the hang of it you will find this very easy to make. So is:

Gumbo

Add a pinch of cayenne for extra heat.

¼ **cup flour**
¼ **cup vegetable oil**
1 package smoked sausage, chopped
1 bag frozen okra
**1 tablespoon Cajun seasoning (I use a little more but it
    gets kinda hot)**
3 cans chicken broth
1 large onion, chopped
3 medium carrots, chopped
1 green pepper (you can use celery), chopped
2 bay leaves

Start by putting the oil and flour in a large pot. THIS IS THE MOST IMPORTANT STEP! Put the heat on medium. Stir this roux CONSTANTLY until it gets to the color that you want your gumbo to be (it will get darker as it cooks). If it gets real black, dump it and start over. Once it gets to the desired color (I like mine tan for gumbo, tan to light brown) add the carrots, onions and green pepper. Sauté for several minutes until the veggies begin to get soft. Add the chicken broth and stir very well. Add the other ingredients. Bring to a boil. Reduce heat and simmer for 30 minutes. Remove the bay leaves. Serve over a bed of rice. (If at any time it gets too thick add a little more broth.) (You can also add shrimp or chicken. If you do, precook the chicken and add it at the time of the other ingredients. If you add shrimp you can put them in raw the last 5 minutes or precook them and add the last two minutes.)

Prep time: 30 minutes. Servings 10.

I heard from many people through the years who have said they won't cook Cajun food because it's so difficult. You will find that like many other dishes, Cajun can be a great cooking experience and can be done by anyone once you have a little experience with it. One of the reasons I love it so much is that it really gives you good kitchen time. I love my kitchen. I feel at home in the kitchen, chopping up vegetables and creating new dishes and very few styles of cooking lend themselves to this any more than Cajun. Do you want to undertake a Cajun dish if you need a quick dish? No. Not many Cajun dishes lend themselves to fast preparation. They are foods of love, and you have to put some love into them. In this case "love" being an hour or more of your time. I like to make these dishes on Sundays when I have lots of time and I can baby my roux and spend time chopping this and that. The flavors need time to marry and have children. No, the dish isn't going to multiply in the pot, but you see the point. It needs time and in some ways time is all we have anyway. Time is on our hands, how we use it is up to us. Another great thing that I really love about Cajun cooking is how it brings the family together. Often times my wife, son and I spend an afternoon putting together a great dish, and usually it's something Cajun. One person can be making a roux while someone else is chopping vegetables and the Dad is drinking coffee and supervising. Actually, I don't pull that off myself but maybe some Dads do. Speaking of pulling off something delicious:

Muffalettas

A sandwich only in appearance, more like a gourmet meal really.

1 loaf French bread
1 lb. salami, thinly sliced
½ lb. prosciutto, thinly sliced
1 lb. provolone cheese, thinly sliced
2 small tomatoes, sliced
½ cup pimento stuffed olives
½ cup pitted kalamata olives
¼ cup olive oil
1 garlic clove
¼ cup roasted red pepper

Place the olives, garlic and peppers in a food processor. Process slowly while adding the oil in a steady stream. Slice the French bread long ways. Spread the olive mixture on both sides of the bread. Layer the salami, prosciutto, provolone and tomatoes on the lower half of the bread. Place the upper half back on and slice into serving size pieces.
Prep time: 20 minutes. Servings: 6.

There are going to be people from Louisiana and elsewhere who say to themselves, "Hey, to be a true Cajun dish that needs this or that," or something along those lines. Some people will say etouffée doesn't have carrots or that fresh garlic is the only kind of garlic you can use. See, that's what I love so much about cooking, it's subjective. If I want my Cajun dishes to have freeze dried garlic only, they will only have freeze dried garlic. I can still call them Cajun because they are my Kentucky version of Cajun. If you have an Indiana version of Cajun, that's great too, as is the Oklahoma version, etc.

What this all means in the greater scope of Muffaletta sandwiches is absolutely nothing, but you will find that this is no normal sandwich. It's a meal in and of itself. A while back we I did a class on Cajun cooking and I must say the Muffaletta sandwich was one of the real hits of the evening. There are not too many times when you think of sandwich and fantastic in the same sentence, but this is one of those times. The olive spread really makes this sandwich, as it will others so make some extra and have it on hand. Toast some bread slices, rub with a garlic clove and spread some of the olive mixture over for a quick snack or simply dip some toast points into it as an appetizer. There are some commercially available varieties available but it only takes a few minutes to make and you will know exactly what is going into it if you do it yourself. Speaking of do it yourself, if you want to spend some time some afternoon getting to know your pots and end up with a knock 'em dead dish try:

Jambalaya

So much flavor all in one pot.

1 lb. chicken thighs (skin on), cut into serving size chunks
1 tablespoon olive oil
2 large onions, coarsely chopped
3 carrots, cut into ½" pieces
1 small green pepper, coarsely chopped
1 small red pepper, coarsely chopped
1 cup brown rice (not Minute rice)
2 cups chicken stock
1 lb. smoked sausage, cut into ½" pieces
2 bay leaves
3 garlic cloves, finely chopped
1 teaspoon Cajun seasoning

Begin by browning the chicken in the oil until well browned on all sides. Remove the chicken and set aside. Add the Trinity (onions, peppers and carrots) to the pot and simmer until the vegetables begin to brown. Add the sausage and the chicken to the pot. Cover and let simmer for 5 minutes. Add all other ingredients including rice and cover. Bring to a boil, then lower temperature to a simmer. Simmer without stirring until liquid is absorbed and rice is tender. Jambalaya gets its color from the chicken and vegetables browning and sticking to the bottom of the pot so allow it to do so. Remove bay leaves and serve.
Prep time: 30 minutes. Servings: 10.

This dish, like most Cajun dishes, is going to take you some time. The great thing about it is that once it gets going you just leave it alone (don't peek) and then come back to it later on. This recipe just begs to be served alongside a nice green salad and some crusty French bread. One comment that I tend to get a lot is that Cajun food is too spicy. If you ever go to my second hometown of New Orleans, or most anywhere in Louisiana and have some good ole-fashioned Cajun food, you will find that it is for the most part very un-spicy. I just created another word which could very well be a record for one cookbook: "un-spicy," meaning not spicy or less than spicy, that's what it is. If you are making it yourself cut down on the Cajun seasoning a little bit and you will happily find the result to be far from spicy. Flavorful is a better term than spicy. One thing you must be willing to expect when you make jambalaya is that it's going to stick to your pot.

Whether your pan is non-stick or not, this dish will stick. Anytime you are cooking Cajun, soups too, for that matter, you are best served using a cast iron pot. Cast iron hold heats extremely well and it heats evenly, thus making it easier to keep things cooking at lower temperatures and cooking them through more efficiently. Another thing to be noted is that a well-seasoned cast iron pot, or a good quality enameled cast iron pot will be very non-stick in its own right. That's not to say that things won't stick to it however; with some care they will last for years. This is far longer than typical pots or skillets and cast iron pots tend to get better the more you use them. If you don't have a cast iron pot don't fret. I have made a ton of wonderful Cajun dishes in regular old pots over the years. Make sure you have a good fitting lid for whichever pot you choose and things will go fine. Since we've got our pots out and on the stove let's make something bold, something that will really get their attention. Something like:

Crawfish Etouffée

If I had to pick one dish to eat forever, this would be it.

⅓ **cup oil (vegetable or olive)**
6 tablespoons flour
1 can chicken stock
1 lb. crawfish tail meat
1 medium onion, chopped
½ **cup chopped carrots, give or take a little**
1 small green pepper, chopped
1 lb. smoked sausage
1 teaspoon Cajun seasoning (I like Slap Your Mama)
1 bag frozen okra (can be omitted if you don't like okra)
3 cloves garlic, chopped
3 bay leaves

Put a large pot on medium and add the oil. Add the flour and stir constantly for 7 to 8 minutes or until it reaches your desired color (I like a medium blonde for mine). Once it reaches the desired color add the onion, carrots and green pepper. Stir and cover and allow to cook for 5 minutes, stirring occasionally. Add the rest of the ingredients except the crawfish meat and bring to a boil. Reduce heat to a simmer. It will be thick, but will thin down some as it cooks. Cook for 35 to 40 minutes (until the veggies are good and soft) then add the crawfish meat. Cook for another 5 minutes. Remove the bay leaves and spoon over rice or serve rice on the side. I like mine really thick, but you can add a little more broth at any time and thin it down a little.
Prep time: 30 minutes. Servings: 10.

So here we have it, bang 'em up etouffée. We are knee deep in the midst of one dish that I could honestly eat every day of my life. Etouffée is one dish that really combines a bunch of great things all in one big gravy covered serving. First you have the gravy, a thick, spicy if you want it to be, covering of tasty goodness. The more of it merrier as far as I'm concerned. Inside this you have those tasty little crawdaddies, all buttered up and ready to rock and roll all the way down to your soul. The combination of those little freshwater delights and the cooked up veggies is almost more than a person can handle but then you realize it's all over that fluffy bed of brown rice and it just takes you to another place culinarily. It truly is a masterpiece and if the person who invented it were here right now I would salute him or her. I would have to salute as I wouldn't be able to speak in the presence of such culinary genius. A quick note: if you don't like crawfish or you can't find them use medium shrimp in their place. I have actually used catfish in place of the crawdaddies but it really takes some babying or it ends up broken into fifty thousand pieces. If you are going to use fish be very delicate with it and add it the last 10 minutes of the cooking time. This will give the fish time to cook and flavor the etouffée without allowing it to fall apart. I have also switched it up and used:

Duck Etouffée

A little heartier version of etouffée.
Have some crusty bread on hand and be hungry.

⅓ cup oil (vegetable or olive)
6 tablespoons flour
16 oz. can chicken stock
2 lbs. duck meat (boneless), cut into 1" pieces
4 tablespoons bacon fat
½ cup flour
1 medium onion, chopped
½ cup chopped carrots (give or take a little)
1 medium red pepper, chopped
1 lb. andouille sausage
1 teaspoon Cajun seasoning (I like Slap Your Mama)
1 bag frozen okra (can be omitted if you don't like okra)
3 cloves garlic, roughly chopped
3 bay leaves

Put a large pot on medium and add the oil. Add 6 tablespoons flour and stir constantly for 7 to 8 minutes or until it reaches your desired color (I like a dark roux for this duck recipe). Once it reaches the desired color add the onion, carrots and red pepper. Stir and cover and allow to cook for 5 minutes, stirring occasionally. Meanwhile in another pot heat bacon fat over medium high heat. In a large Ziploc bag place ½ cup flour and the duck pieces. Shake well to coat. In small batches add the duck meat to the bacon fat and brown thoroughly on all sides. Add the duck to the vegetables and add the rest of the ingredients. Reduce heat to a simmer. It will be thick, but will thin up some as it cooks. Cook for 35 to 40 minutes until the veggies are good and soft. Remove the bay leaves and spoon over rice or serve rice on the side. I like mine really thick, but you can add a little more broth at any time and thin it down a little.
Prep time: 30 minutes. Servings: 10.

We are now in a different place in this book. A place we haven't gone. Up until now most everything has been different in some way from the previous recipe but here we have two recipes with basically the same name and same preparation techniques. The resemblance ends right there however, as they couldn't be more different in the finished product. The duck etouffée is bold, has a depth that the crawfish doesn't and really benefits from a dark roux that brings out the all the earthy goodness that wild game (you can use store bought duck or goose if you can't get your hands on wild ones) provides. Like most wild game, duck and goose tends to be coarse with strong lines in the meat and has very little fat. That being the case it needs to be cooked in different ways than people are used to as far as beef or pork is concerned. A steak can be bought, brought home and placed on the grill until it's well done and still eaten without gagging. Most wild game cannot and duck is no exception to that. It needs quick flash cooking to medium rare or a long slow cooking process like this etouffée to really bring out its highlights.

Now that our bellies are completely stuffed to the point that we have to start wondering if our belts got wet and shrunk, let's change gears a bit.

Soup's On

It may be crossing your mind at this point in the book that we have not covered any starters. We went straight into superbly filling side dishes and rib sticking main courses without ever setting foot in a bowl of soup. All that, my friends, is about to change. First I would like to say this: to think that every meal must be served in the order of salad or soup, main course and then dessert is to fall into the trappings of food society. As I said earlier, it's up to you what you serve, how you serve it and when you serve it. So many times I find myself saying, "Rats ear, I can't believe I didn't set the Reuben dip out prior to the barbecued brisket!!" This is, of course, just a scenario and not something word for word that I typically would say, but you get the point. The point is if I'm cooking and I'm serving I can do it in any fashion that I choose. Is someone going to get upset that I didn't follow some protocol for how I managed to get the food into the stomach? Perhaps they will but that doesn't mean I am going to get upset about it. If I want to (or simply do it because I forgot) to serve my soup last I by golly will do so. It's called individualism and it's not a bad thing. There are many times at home when I eat my salad last and my dessert first. That doesn't make me a bad person, it simply makes me my own person. Anyone who's been to one of my cooking classes can attest to this. I cook it and serve it like I want to and if I go to someone's house to eat I expect them to do the same. It's really all about the food, not about the order it comes in. All this talk of how and when has gotten me to thinking about:

Pork Stew

I love this hearty soup on rainy days.

**1 package boneless pork loin or boneless pork chops,
  cut into ½" pieces**
1 can corn
1 package frozen okra
1 large onion, chopped
1 64 oz. can tomato juice
1 tablespoon Italian seasoning
2 large potatoes, chopped
Salt and pepper

Cook pork and onions in a large pot until almost cooked through and onions are starting to get tender. Add the other ingredients and bring to a boil. Simmer for 30 minutes or until potatoes are tender.
Prep time: 20 minutes. Servings: 10.

As I look back on this recipe, which I have made a hundred times through the years, I can't help but think of how easy it is to prepare. You can see by the instructions on how to prepare it that the simplicity of it screams at you. It's very filling and in a lot of ways reminds me of vegetable soup. Pork is a really nice change up and lends a little different consistency than you get with chicken or beef. The okra gives it a real down south feel while the potatoes give it depth. It's fairly hearty and really hits the spot on cold days, in a way almost like a runnier chili. Runnier, meaning more runny than standard runny; an advanced runny stage. Am I the only one that finds stages of runny funny? Perhaps, but I am moving on to one of my absolute favorite soups:

16 Bean Soup

My wife's wonderful, filling soup.

1 package 16 bean soup mix
4 cups chicken stock
½ teaspoon garlic powder
½ teaspoon chili powder
½ teaspoon black pepper
½ teaspoon smoked sea salt
1 lb. andouille sausage, cut into ½" pieces
1 medium size onion, roughly chopped
1 green pepper, roughly chopped

Soak beans for 24 hours. This is very important as this is what lends to having exceptionally tender soup. Rinse beans twice. Place beans in a large pot. Add stock and all spices (except the spice packet that came with the beans) the onions and peppers. Bring to a boil and simmer for 1 hour. Add the sausage and bring back to a simmer. Continue to simmer for 45 minutes or until beans and veggies are very tender.
Prep time: 30 minutes. Servings: 12.

Being the fine man that I am, it's only right for me to give credit where credit is due here. My wife originally made this recipe and I just tailored it a smidge. Being as how I like a thicker, more stew-like soup, I do on occasion add a little cornstarch to it and get a little more gravy-like consistency. The great thing about this soup is that once it gets going it really requires very little maintenance. Beans as a whole do take some time when getting ready, but the overnight soaking is not a tedious process so it really sounds worse than it is. Anytime you tell someone they need to do something the night before they begin to worry. Trust me, you will make this soup perfectly the first time you make it. You could use some beef or vegetable stock if you didn't have chicken stock on hand, but chicken really fits perfectly with this dish. The spices bring just a slight kick and the andouille balances out the softness and flavor of the beans. This may not be the perfect soup, but if its not it sure ain't far away. Another soup that may just be teetering on the sidelines of perfection is:

Italian Sausage and Lentil Soup

Another recipe that came from a night out and some trial and error.

8 oz. dried lentils
8 oz. dried barley
24 oz. beef broth
1 cup carrots, chopped into small pieces
1 medium onion, chopped into ¼" pieces
1 lb. bulk Italian sausage
2 cloves garlic, finely chopped
½ teaspoon rubbed sage
Salt and pepper to taste
3 tablespoons cornstarch
½ cup water

Mix cornstarch and water and set aside. Cook lentils and barley according to package direction. In a large saucepan crumble the Italian Sausage. Add the carrots, onions, and sage. Cook over medium heat until sausage is cooked through. Drain any grease and return meat and vegetables to pan. Add the beef broth and bring to a simmer. Simmer for 20 minutes. Add garlic and cornstarch mixture to soup. Return to a simmer. Simmer for 5 minutes or until thickened.
Prep time: 20 minutes. Servings: 10.

Shawn Keeton, author and chef.

Grilled Salmon
(recipe on page 25)

Veggies by the pond.

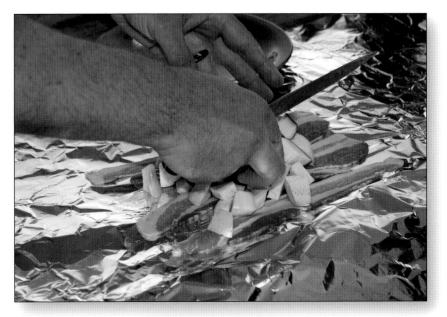

Grilled Summer Veggies
(recipe on page 28)

Grilled Salmon with Summer Veggies.

A happy family.

Zucchini Boats
(recipe on page 30)

Stuffed Meatloaf
(recipe on page 46)

Tomato Insalata with Balsamic Reduction
(recipe on page 63)

Orzo Pasta with Black Beans
(recipe on page 68)

Chilaquiles
(recipe on page 74)

Spanish Rice
(recipe on page 77)

Mexican Salad
(recipe on page 78)

Jambalaya
(recipe on page 87)

Borscht
(recipe on page 114)

Chili Seasonings
(recipe on page 119)

Minestrone
(recipe on page 122)

Turkey Confit
(recipe on page 138)

Shawn Keeton in the kitchen with son, Clay.

Chocolate Chip Cheeseball
(recipe on page 142)

Zucchini Bread
(recipe on page 143)

Family, friends and food are what make life great.

Boys and girls, this little jewel right here is a home run in any ballpark. I came up with this recipe after having a similar soup in a restaurant one night. My wife said at the time, "This is wonderful, do you think you can make something similar?" My reply of course was, "No, I can make something better," and this baby was born. I nurtured her like an infant and after a few improvements I lay her at your feet (actually your mouths) here today. This soup has it all: a wonderful broth base that really adds to the flavors without overpowering anything, Italian sausage and all the great spices it brings, lentils and barley for heartiness and carrots for wonderful color. This is another soup that I like to thicken a little right at the very end. Make sure your cornstarch (or flour or arrowroot) is completely smooth before you add it to the soup so you don't end up with little floating funkies in there. This soup is a meal in itself, so if you add some nice garlic bread and a small salad you'll have some happy eaters. If you are going to serve this as a traditional soup beginning the meal, cut the portions down. The lentil and barley tend to fill people up fast and a big bowl of this won't leave much room for other courses. Like most soups, this is best if you make it ahead of time and let the flavors marry, say a day or so before you are going to serve it, but make sure you have some extra stock on hand when you re-heat it. This soup tends to get thicker overnight as the lentils and barley absorb more liquid. Now that's you've hit a recipe out of the park, I'll let you in on another that may not be a home run every time, but it's a triple no matter who's at bat:

Borscht

It should be more common than it is.

2 quarts beef stock
3 tablespoons butter
1 cup cabbage, finely chopped
1 cup potatoes, chopped
½ cup carrots, chopped
1 onion, chopped
1½ cups canned tomatoes
½ cup juice (from can of beets)
1 cup cooked or canned beets, chopped
1 teaspoon vinegar
Sour cream
Fresh dill (optional)
Salt and pepper to taste

In a large heavy pan, melt butter and lightly sauté cabbage, potatoes, carrots and onion for approximately 5 minutes. Add beef stock. Blend canned tomatoes or press through a sieve until fine. Add puréed tomatoes and beet juice to stock. Cover and simmer over low heat until vegetables are tender but not soft. At this point, add the chopped beets and vinegar. Season well with salt and pepper and remove from heat before the beets begin to lose their color. Serve with a dollop of sour cream and a sprinkling of dill or parsley over each bowl.
Prep time: 20 minutes. Servings: 10.

After viewing this recipe I feel certain some people are rolling their eyes. After all, borscht is not quite a household word in this country. I find this to be pretty odd in a lot of ways especially considering how popular it is in many other countries. I have been served this in many different fashion overseas and have loved all of them. Beets tend to be pretty popular in this good ole USofA as well, so it's even more perplexing that it hasn't really become a staple of our cuisine. Before I go on to rave how good this is I will say that you probably need to like beets, or at least not detest them, before you try this recipe. It certainly has a beet flair about it as well as the gorgeous color that the cooked beets lend to it. Day in and day out this is one of the prettiest dishes you will serve. It's a lighter soup which makes it ideal to serve a bit of before a heavy meal, unlike the previous couple of soups I listed. The flavors of the beets and cabbage really reach out and grab your tongue in a twisting motion, a good twisting, and don't let go. Potatoes and carrots add some zeal to the finished product, but I'm not going to lie: the beets and cabbage are the heart and soul of this soup. If you have light colored serving bowls this is the place to use them as this soup sparkles against a light background. Have some fresh snipped dill and sour cream on hand when you serve it and not only does the flavor smack you in the face, it takes the already great presentation to another level. Speaking of going to another level:

The World's Best Veggie Soup

According to my own rankings.

2 14 oz. cans chicken broth
2 cups water
2 large baking potatoes, cut into ¾" cubes
3 large carrots, cut into ½" slices
1 can black beans, drained and rinsed
1 can Ro-Tel
1 bag frozen sweet corn
1 bag frozen green beans
1 bag frozen peas and carrots
1 medium size chuck roast, cut into ½" cubes
1 64 oz. can tomato juice
1 teaspoon Italian seasonings
¼ teaspoon garlic powder
Salt and pepper to taste

Place the roast in either a slow cooker for several hours or in a pressure cooker for 20 minutes or until the meat is tender.
In a large sauce pan add the chicken broth and bring to a boil. Add the potatoes and carrots and cook for 5 minutes. Veggies will not be cooked through. Add all ingredients including roast, potatoes, carrots and broth to a large pot. Bring all to a simmer. Add the water. There should be enough liquid to make it very soupy, if there's not add some more water. Bring to a boil, then turn the heat down to simmer. Simmer stirring occasionally for 30 minutes or until all vegetables are very tender. Allow to sit for 30 minutes for flavors to incorporate.
Prep time: 30 minutes. Servings: 10.

The first thing you will probably notice is the title of this recipe. The truth is that this soup has not won any awards certifying it as the world's best. That being said, it has not lost any of the same awards so it could very well be the world's best and I just don't know it, therefore I titled it that just in case it actually is. "What makes this the world's best?" you are probably wondering. Well, I have an answer for that actually: the real key lies in using stock for your base instead of water. There is, of course, water in it, but the addition of the stock really brings a feel to this soup. I call it having bottom. Instead of just a plain ole-run-of-the-mill soup, it now has a feel about it. It's like a good Blues song; it touches the inside of you. Of course, you can use other stocks that you might have on hand; I just tend to reach for chicken when I want real flavor and not overpowering. Beyond that, the vegetables are really what make the soup. Sure, it has beef in it as well but that's just the opening act. The headliner is the vegetables. If you have fresh vegetables you can really take this soup to another level, however the seasonings and spices make canned or frozen veggies a great alternative, especially during the winter months when fresh is hard to come by. This is truly a soup that there should be a penalty for if you eat it the same day, maybe a fine or perhaps a night in the grey bar hotel. I am being serious here; you are never going to get the true feel of this soup if you eat it the day it's made. Have another dish on standby that you can eat the day you make this so you're not too tempted to dig in. The vegetables need time to soak up the broth and spices. It's like love: it needs time to develop to really be appreciated. Always think, veggie soup equals love and you will be just fine. To really bring this recipe up a level add a teaspoon of red pepper flakes and let it set. Whooo weeee, now you're talking lip smackin' soup.

Speaking of lip smackin' soups, it's now time for the one and only, the go to winter soup for most all people, yes it's:

Best Bowl of Red

A full blown party thrown on the taste buds.

2 lbs. chuck roast, cut into ½" cubes
1 cup all purpose flour
1 large onion, chopped
1 green pepper, chopped
3 tablespoons olive oil
2 cans black beans
2 cans diced tomatoes
6 cups tomato juice
1 teaspoon oregano
3 teaspoons chili seasoning (see recipe below)
2 cloves garlic, minced
Hot sauce (optional)
Sour cream (optional)
Shredded cheese (optional)

Place the flour in a resealable bag. Add the chuck and shake to coat. Place the olive oil in a large dutch oven (or large pot). Add meat (several batches at a time if it gets too full) and brown on all sides. Add all ingredients and bring to a simmer. Simmer for 45 minutes or until meat and onions are tender. Taste and adjust seasonings if necessary.
Prep time: 20 minutes. Servings: 10.

I am almost sweating just thinking about it. Red is in the head. This is really just chili but I like to call it red, as it has a red look and consists of red chilies, tomatoes etc. I love me some red, oh boy do I. The addition of chuck makes this recipe the real go-to of all my soup recipes. Sure, other ones have beef in them, but none has the combination of beef, beans, spices and tomatoes that all add up to make this so special. This has bite, character and finish and every bit of it shows in every bite. Often times you'll find soups or just foods in general that have a good element or two, but not all of them at the same time. This baby rocks it all from beginning to end and is just as good 10 minutes after its ready as it is two days later. The thing is there are no vegetables to soak up flavors in that overnight, time consuming manner. The meat cooks with the seasonings and is simply drenched in all their thick, spicy goodness. You can really spice this up nicely with the addition of a jalapeno cut up and put into the chili at the same time you add the meat. The great thing about adding a jalapeno is you can make it less spicy by discarding the seeds and more spicy by adding the seeds. Little things like adding the seeds of a jalapeno can be real time savers in the kitchen and great little tricks for changing up a recipe if you've made it several times and want to get a new feel from the dish. When it comes to chili, you can buy chili spices or you can simply make up a mix of your own and keep it on hand. For many years now I have been using:

Chili Seasonings
Save some money by making this in bulk and storing in sealable plastic bags.

¼ cup seasoned salt
¼ cup garlic powder
¼ cup cumin
4 tablespoons black powder
4 tablespoons oregano
4 tablespoons ground Anaheim or New Mexico chilies
1 teaspoon cayenne pepper

Mix all ingredients and store in a tightly sealed bowl or Ziploc bag.
Prep time: 10 minutes.

This mix of spices is a wonderful way to always have some chili seasonings on hand and also goes great in scrambled eggs. Experiment a little with the amount of cayenne until you find the heat level you like. You will find that black pepper tends to spice things up a bit, but the real heat here is coming from the cayenne. You can now find ground chili peppers of many varieties in specialty stores. Try adding some of these to your mix for a special flavor. Chipotle will add smokiness and zesty spice while Anaheim chilies will add more of a spicy flair.

When we talk about chili powder, a lot of people think of canned chili powder. Chili powder in the can is not just ground-up chilies, it is a mix of chilies, oregano, garlic and sometimes other spices such as black pepper. I like to use ground chilies, not chili powder simply because I want to add my own amount of flavorful spices and not rely on what someone else has measured and placed in a can. If you grow your own chilies, simply dry them and using a mortar and pestle, grind them to a powder. I briefly spoke earlier about how the influx of new cultures has affected our food availability and this is another example of what I was meaning. If you have your own garden or grow peppers in pots you have a great availability of seeds to start. If you live in a cold weather area, try growing them indoors as they tend to be very easy to get going. Most years I lament the fact that I planted so many. While I am on the subject of using spices and things that are easily grown, it reminds of this great summer recipe:

Tomato Soup with Rosemary and Cilantro

If you don't want to chop the rosemary,
put it in cheesecloth and remove after cooking.

3 lbs. Roma tomatoes, chopped
1 medium sweet onion, finely chopped
1 cup tomato juice
¼ cup fresh cilantro, chopped
1 small sweet pepper, finely chopped
4 tablespoons fresh rosemary leaves, finely chopped
Juice from one lemon
¾ teaspoon sugar
Very cold water

Place the tomatoes in a large pot with just enough water to cover. Boil for 10 minutes, drain then add onions, tomato juice, sweet pepper, lemon juice and sugar in a blender. Puree for 30 seconds, stir and repeat for another 30 seconds. This will need to be done in several batches. Mix well once all the ingredients are blended. Pour into a large bowl. If you want a very smooth soup, strain it and remove the solids. Add enough of the cold water to make it more soup like. Stir in cilantro and rosemary and refrigerate for several hours to overnight. Spoon into bowls and serve chilled.

Prep time: 20 minutes. Servings: 10.

I made this awesome cold soup in a cooking class one time and it was a huge hit. Looking back on the borscht recipe reminds me that this is another style of soup that gets very little love in this country. We are simply not into cold soups for the most part and after you taste this hopefully you will be a convert. The mix of fresh tomatoes and garden vegetables really makes this soup refreshing, almost like standard gazpacho, a common cold soup in South America. I called for Roma tomatoes in the recipe, however if you raise a different variety in your garden or can only find a certain variety at the local farmers market, then by all means use them. Romas tend to hold up a little better to cooking, but in this recipe they are being pureed anyway so go right ahead and use whatever variety you have on hand. The fresh rosemary and cilantro in this dish take the flavors to a different level. Rosemary adds a wonderful woodsy earthiness, while cilantro adds bite and that distinctive flavor of southwest cuisine.

When I first started trying to grow cilantro I decided to grow some beside our house. I roughed up the ground a little bit and scattered some seeds. For the next four years I had so much cilantro I didn't know what to do with all of it. I live in northern Kentucky, and our temperature seems to be very good for herbs to grow. I have made the mistake several times of planting herbs in the garden, in our flower garden and along our outside walls and without fail they all take over and grow almost out of control, returning each spring. I love herbs for sure, having them sprout every two inches in my garden, I don't really love all that much. All soups of course don't need herbs to be delicious. An example of this is:

Minestrone

Pasta adds depth and character to this beautiful soup.

3 tablespoons olive oil
1 large sweet onion, chopped
1 tablespoon tomato paste
8 oz. whole wheat elbow pasta
1 lb. Roma tomatoes, chopped
1 medium zucchini, chopped
1 medium yellow squash, chopped
2 small red potatoes, chopped
2 garlic cloves, minced
6 cups chicken stock
6 tablespoons fresh basil, roughly chopped
Parmesan cheese to taste

Heat the oil in a large pot. Add the onion and cook until softened but not browned. Add the tomato paste and potatoes. Cook for 10-12 minutes, stirring often. Add the garlic, tomatoes, whole wheat pasta, zucchini, squash and stock and bring to a simmer. Simmer for 15 minutes or until vegetables and noodles are tender. Remove from heat and add the basil. Put into serving bowls and sprinkle with the cheese.
Prep time: 20 minutes. Servings: 10.

Here we see a soup that I make often that utilizes vegetables and pasta. Pasta tends to be limited to sauces, but it really shines in soups as well. Often times it's served in chili and vegetable soup, in which it lends a nice texture and makes dishes very filling. This minestrone is a very nice soup to serve to friends and family as it makes large quantities and is not overly spiced. One thing that tends to make parties and get-togethers not go so well is over spiced foods. If you know your crowd well, feel free to serve zesty food full of flavors and complicated tastes; if you don't, it's best to keep things simple and less spicy. I used to think that because I loved spicy food, so did everyone else. It doesn't take many times serving huge pots of food only to see most all of it left in the pot to realize that's not the case. All of the vegetables in this soup are light flavored as well. Zucchini, yellow squash, potatoes and so on typically don't turn people off, and the Parmesan adds just enough flavor without becoming overpowering. I like to take this soup outside, as it makes a great evening meal outdoors with friends or family. Pair this soup with a nice green salad and white wine and let the kids play. I can't think of many better ways to spend an evening then with good company and children playing in the yard. Another recipe that really comes to mind when I think of having company over doesn't fit the bill of soup, but I couldn't think of any place that it fit better than right here:

Tomato Gravy

Sauce for those who aren't comfortable calling it gravy.

14 oz. chicken stock (other stocks such as beef and duck will work)
6 oz. tomato paste
1 tablespoon each fresh oregano and thyme
14 oz. diced tomatoes
6 oz. onion, roughly chopped
6 oz. mushrooms, roughly chopped
½ cup Merlot or dry red wine
2 oz. real butter
2 garlic cloves, minced
3 teaspoons cornstarch
Salt and pepper to taste

Heat a large sauce pan on medium heat. Add the stock, tomato paste and herbs. Cover and bring to a simmer. Allow to simmer for 20 minutes to blend flavors. In a medium saucepan add the butter and onions and mushrooms. Sauté for 5 minutes. Add the Merlot and continue to sauté until wine has reduced by half and vegetables are tender. Add the diced tomatoes to the stock and bring it back to a boil. Using a potato masher, smash the tomatoes to whatever coarseness you prefer (you can blend this in small batches if you prefer a smoother sauce). Add the wine and vegetables to the pot. Add the garlic. Let the gravy simmer for 5 minutes. Meanwhile, add just enough water to the cornstarch to make a smooth paste. Add the cornstarch in small amounts until gravy reaches the desired thickness, allowing it to boil between each addition.
Prep time: 15 minutes.

I use this sauce a ton. I find myself making this in large batches and freezing it for use later, as well as making it the day I want to use it and simply tossing it with whole wheat noodles or putting over cooked chicken breasts and placing in the oven for a few minutes until hot and bubbly. I prefer to use fresh tomatoes; however, we have a short season here for good ripe tomatoes and I don't stop making this sauce simply because the availability of tasty tomatoes drops. If you have some fresh tomatoes on hand, by all means use them. It's best to place them in some boiling water for a minute or so and remove the skins before proceeding on with the recipe, but they will lend a great flavor that only fresh tomatoes can. Now that we've souped ourselves up and worked into a food frenzy, let's move on to one of my most beloved styles of food.

Startin' Off Right

I have already said many times in this cookbook I love just about all foods. I can eat vegetarian, I love meat, soups are wonderful on cool days and hearty casseroles really hit the spot when you're just downright hungry. Of all food categories, however, I love appetizers the best. I could honestly eat appetizers and dips and other snack foods for every meal, without accompanying dishes. I love the consistency of dips, creamy and warm, sometimes spicy. The contrast that comes from cream cheese and crackers is one that you don't find in many styles of food other than appetizers. That's not to say that cream cheese is the only dip ingredient of course, but often times when I want to create a special starter I find myself reaching for cream cheese before any other ingredient. It's very versatile and won't overpower your other ingredients while still giving foods a bit of a taste lift. The other great thing about cream cheese is that it melts extremely well. Some cheeses tend not to melt well at all so keep this in mind when selecting a base for your dish. From a base of cheese you can easily go one of a hundred ways: spicy, extra cheesy, sour, hearty and more. I often get asked the question, "How did you come up with that recipe?" The answer to that question, especially when concerning finger foods, often times lies in the selection of cream cheese as a base ingredient. The following recipe is an example of just that process, (see tip #22 for appetizer servings):

Country Ham and Swiss Cheese Dip

Salt cured ham gives this dip an extra special bite.

8 oz. thin sliced country ham
2 8 oz. packages cream cheese, softened
8 oz. shredded swiss cheese
2 tablespoons coarse ground mustard
Dash of garlic powder

Heat a skillet over medium flame and add country ham slices. Sauté for 2 minutes per side and remove from heat. Coarsely chop ham and set aside. In a large mixing bowl combine cream cheese, swiss cheese, mustard and garlic. Fold in country ham. Place all in a slow cooker and heat on high for 40 minutes or until hot and bubbly. Serve with melba toasts or other strong crackers. Prep time: 15 minutes.

Here we see a recipe that I created on a moment's notice before going to a Christmas dinner. Later in this cookbook I am going to highlight a few things I like to have on hand at all times and you will see how easy it was to make this dip. It's a very simple and quick fix and the combination of smooth and salty foods make it a real hit. I received a ton of compliments on this dish with most wondering how it came about. Little did they know it was 10 minutes in my kitchen just before heading to the dinner. Another dip that came about, and was taken to the same dinner the year before, really comes to mind here. It's another super easy dish that will really knock their socks off:

Pizza Dip

All the flavor of your favorite pizza in an easy to serve dip.

1 pepperoni roll (or 2 packages pepperonis), cut into ¼" pieces

2 small cans sliced black olives, drained
2 jars pizza sauce (you could make your own and it
   would be even better)
1 large onion, chopped
1 green pepper, chopped
1 package sliced mushrooms
½ teaspoon oregano
½ teaspoon thyme
16 oz. shredded mozzarella cheese
2 tablespoon butter

In a large skillet, sauté the onions, pepper and mushrooms in the butter over medium heat until tender (about 5 minutes). Sprinkle with the oregano and thyme. Set to the side. In a large bowl mix the black olives, pepperonis, pizza sauce and cheese. Fold in the onion mixture and place all in a large baking dish (a crock pot works well also). Place in a 400 degree oven for 20 minutes or until hot and bubbly.
Prep time: 20 minutes.

Pizza dip is one of the finest things, culinarily, that you will ever put in your mouth, as long as you like pizza or pizza flavored foods. This is one dip that truly has it all and is a flavor explosion. Your tongue almost feels like it is going to blow up right in your mouth. The zesty flavor of the pizza sauce melds in perfect harmony with the spiciness of the pepperonis, while the oregano and thyme forge their own cut of the sensory organs. Mozzarella gives this dip creaminess, while the onions, peppers and mushrooms add flavor and texture. You will notice that there is no cream cheese in this dip. With the pizza sauce as a base, there is no need to bulk this up by using cream cheese. I have made it in the past using 8 ounces of cheddar cheese in addition to the mozzarella, however the benefits as far as flavor go don't really go up that much. Make no mistake, this recipe doesn't need anything to help it along. It's a stand-alone grand slam and one that will surely get many comments from your crowd. Along the same lines, only in a spicy way, is another dip that I make often. As a matter of fact I made it just a week ago while we were watching football games on television:

Buffalo Chicken Dip

Spicy, filling and fun, a perfect game day dip.

**3 boneless, skinless chicken breasts or 2 large cans
   white chicken meat**
8 oz. cream cheese, softened
½ cup chunky bleu cheese dressing
½ cup crumbled bleu cheese
6 oz. hot sauce (or to taste)
6 oz. shredded mozzarella cheese
6 oz. shredded Monterrey jack cheese

Heat oven to 350 degrees. Cook and shred chicken (or shred canned chicken). Add dressing, hot sauce, celery and chicken and mix well. Add cheddar cheese and pour into a greased baking dish. Bake for 30 minutes or until bubbly. Serve with chips or crackers.
Prep time: 15 minutes.

Looking at this awesome spicy dip we see that once again we are back to incorporating cream cheese in a dip. I believe that anytime you are using chicken in a dip, cream cheese fits perfectly with it. Chicken, or beef for that matter, really benefits from the texture that cream cheese adds to a dish. The coarseness that meat brings to a dish is offset by having smooth consistencies thrown in for balance. The main flavor you are going to get from this dip is the hot sauce. Keep in mind that anytime you add powerful ingredients, hot sauce and blue cheese in this instance, they are going to outweigh the other lesser components in the dish. I talked earlier about herbs doing this exact same thing. Not only do herbs add to a dish, they can become the signature flavor of that same dish and we see that here. With almost certainty you can say that the blue cheese and the hot sauce are going to define each bite. If you don't want it to be as spicy, vary the type of hot sauce you use. There are many good sauces that come in fairly low on the Scoville scale. The Scoville scale is the standard measurement of hot peppers and their heat. Sometimes you will see Scoville units printed on the side of a bottle. If you want to stay below what most people consider to be "hot," you need to find one that is below 1200 on the Scoville scale. There are many that fit this bill perfectly but try starting with green sauces or garlic sauces. Typically these are not as hot as red sauces as they contain other ingredients that help tone down the peppers. One appetizer that I really can't get enough of falls far from the spicy tree and it's a cinch to make:

Bruschetta

It's hard to believe this much flavor comes from this little time and effort.

1 French Bread loaf
1 lb. Roma tomatoes, chopped
3 cloves garlic, finely chopped
½ cup olive oil
¼ cup fresh basil leaves, finely chopped
½ cup shredded Parmesan cheese

Combine tomatoes, garlic and basil in a bowl. Place in the refrigerator for several hours. Preheat oven on broil. Cut French bread crossways into ½" thick slices. Brush lightly with olive oil and place on a cookie sheet. Put into the hot oven and brown bread lightly. Turn bread over and lightly brown on the other side. Remove from oven and place a tablespoon (or slightly more) on top of each bread slice, spreading a little to cover the bread. Sprinkle with cheese and place back into oven for 1 minute or just until cheese begins to melt. Serve immediately.
Prep time: 15 minutes.

One thing that makes a recipe truly great in my book is if it can be made ahead of time so that on game day I'm not rushing around trying to put everything together. Bruschetta is a perfect example of a snack like this. It's super easy to make and the tomato mixture can be made the day before, placed in a bowl with a good fitting lid and kept in the refrigerator. The only thing that's needed the day of is to make the toasts and assemble and it's ready to eat. Ease is the key word here, but don't think for a minute that the flavor is not outstanding. It's a knockout with the fresh basil and tomatoes and makes a great starter for an Italian dinner, or just to go alongside some dips and such at a party. One such dip that I really love to take to special occasions is:

Slow Cooker Reuben Dip

A classic dip that is as easy to make as it is delicious.

1 lb. thinly sliced corned beef, roughly chopped
8 oz. shredded swiss cheese
1 15 oz. can sauerkraut
¾ cup thousand dressing
1 tablespoon caraway seeds

Mix all ingredients in slow cooker. Cook on high power for 1 hour or until hot and bubbly throughout. Stir well and serve with crackers, preferably Triscuits or rye toasts.
Prep time: 15 minutes.

We start to see a pattern here with the use of certain ingredients, but also with the use of the slow cooker. I must confess that I am not the world biggest slow cooker fan. They are nice for making tough cuts of meat edible and are fine for days when the stress level may be high and dinner would not get fixed otherwise. Where I think they really shine is with dips and other appetizers that need to be kept warm over an extended period of time. If you have electric you can pretty much be assured that a slow cooker will keep things at a temperature fit for serving without scorching, especially if you purchase a slow cooker with "serve" or "keep warm" setting. This low temperature setting is perfect for these cheese based, creamy dips as it keeps the cheese melted without burning it to a crisp. The Reuben dip is a classic recipe and one that totally resembles the sandwich, only easier to eat and a cinch to prepare. I have served this dip many times in the past to people who say, "I'm not a sauerkraut fan," and to a person they love the dip. I honestly believe that a good number of people are turned off by the strong tasting rye bread that most Reubens are served on, they like the dip because it is served on a medium, a cracker in this case, that they like. I call this dip a classic, because it fits my mode of what true classic dishes should be. It's hearty, flavorful and can be served before or during a meal, almost acting as a side dish. Another classic dip that I truly love is:

Artichoke Dip

A true classic.

2 cans quartered artichokes, chopped into small pieces
**1 package frozen spinach, drained and squeezed to
    remove liquid**
**½ cup roasted red peppers, drained and roughly
    chopped**
3 cups mayonnaise
⅔ cup Parmesan cheese

Mix all ingredients. Place in an oven proof dish or slow cooker and bake on 350 degrees for 20 minutes or until lightly browned on top. Serve with Triscuits or other crackers.
Prep time: 10 minutes.

Most people who are any kind of dip fans at all have been around artichoke dip for many years. This is a classic simply because of its longevity. I have seen artichoke dip served a thousand times and almost without fail it tastes similar to the last one, even though it may have been made by a totally different person in a totally different setting. The method of preparation involving some light knife work and a serving bowl or slow cooker couldn't be any easier for a dish with this much flavor. Oddly enough, I get more comments about artichokes than any other food I serve. Artichokes are still a relative unknown to many people, especially in rural areas. Growing up I can't ever remember even seeing a can of artichokes, much less hearing of anyone buying a fresh one and cooking it. My wife has a lot to do with me developing a love for them, as she grew up eating them. This illustrates that artichokes truly are a more urban type of food, at least in the part of the country where I reside. The addition of roasted peppers (see the tips section for how to's on roasted peppers) really brings a nice flair to the dip. In and of itself artichoke dip tends to be very bland looking so the red peppers really stand out against the lighter background of the mayonnaise and artichokes. They lend their own slightly acidic bite to the dish. I have had this dish served with various cheeses and even with celery, however I find it best to keep it simple and good. People tend to like things that are simple and tasty, which is why most people I serve this to love it:

Hot Crab Dip
A nice, lightly flavored dip with zest.

1 package imitation crab meat, chopped, or 2 cans crab meat
8 oz. cream cheese, softened
1 pint sour cream

1 teaspoon cayenne pepper (less if you don't want it spicy)
1 small onion, chopped
½ green pepper, chopped
8 oz. shredded cheddar cheese
Salt and pepper to taste
½ teaspoon garlic powder

Mix all ingredients and refrigerate overnight. Serve with crackers or small pieces of toast.
Prep time: 10 minutes.

I developed this dip several years back after trying some similar dips at parties I had been to. This crab dip has many great flavors, but what you find when you make it is they all fit together in fine balance. None of the ingredients overpower the others and all sit together, not fighting amongst themselves for popularity on your taste buds. You can alter the flavor of this dip significantly by simply adding more or less garlic powder and cayenne powder. Almost without fail there are a few ingredients in every dish that can totally change the flavor and depth of the dish by simply adding a little or taking away a little. We see this even in recipes that have numerous ingredients. Knowing which ones are the standouts really helps you tailor the dish to your liking, and hopefully to that of your friends and families. As I said earlier in the book, don't let the dislike for an ingredient or two stop you from trying a recipe. Feel confident in your ability to substitute a flavor that you like more and go with it. If it doesn't turn out like you expect it to, keep trying. Persistence is the best friend of a good cook. It's always easier to file sixty-nine, throw away, a recipe rather than tailor it to fit your tastes. You will surely feel better if you take a recipe and make it your own. One recipe that is a true testament to this is:

Antipasta with Vinaigrette
Vary the meats and cheeses you use
for a different flair each time you serve this.

6 roasted peppers, different colors
½ cup sun dried tomatoes, chopped
1 cup mixed olives in oil, chopped
1 small can artichoke hearts, drained and chopped
½ cup pepperoncinis, sliced
6 tablespoons balsamic vinegar (red wine vinegar will work as well)
2 garlic cloves, minced
1 cup olive oil
Dash of hot sauce (optional)

Using a whisk mix the olive oil, balsamic vinegar, garlic and hot sauce. Set aside. Roughly chop the roasted peppers and add the tomatoes, olives, artichoke hearts and pepperoncinis in a large bowl. Drizzle with the dressing.
Prep time: 15 minutes.

Over the years I have had many different antipastas, some good and some not so good. The basic translation of antipasta is, "before the meal," that is a serving of food preceding the meal itself. Typically antipastas are a selection of cured meats, olives and other things served at the table prior to a meal. In this case, I took many of the things that I liked about traditional antipastas and added something that I really like, in this case a vinaigrette. After that I tossed it all together to make a dish that's really outstanding. The colors and flavors of this dish get together wonderfully, and it can become a meal of its own if served over torn up leaf lettuce. I often find myself looking to include sun dried tomatoes more in my daily cooking and they go perfectly in this antipasta. The texture selection and beautiful colors of the ingredients make this dish as lovely to look at as it is to eat. I like to serve it in a big white bowl, which really brings the color to life. Put all of your meats and vegetables together the day before and toss with the vinaigrette just before serving. Make sure you have plenty of copies of the recipe on hand as you will surely get requests for it. Another recipe that I get lots of comments on is:

Hot Crab Pinwheels

Perfect for making ahead of time. Refrigerate and serve the following day.

8 oz. cream cheese
1 6 oz. can crabmeat, drained and cartilage removed
¾ cup finely chopped sweet red pepper
½ cup shredded cheddar cheese
2 green onions, finely chopped
3 tablespoons fresh parsley, minced
¼-½ teaspoon cayenne pepper
6 6" flour tortillas (I used the larger ones and it still made 6-8 rolls)

Heat oven to 350 degrees. In a bowl beat the cream cheese until smooth. Stir in the crab, red pepper, cheese, onions, parsley and cayenne. Spread ⅓ cup over 1 side of each tortilla. Roll up tightly and wrap with plastic wrap. Refrigerate for at least 2 hours. Cut roll ups into 1" wide pieces discarding the ends. Place on a baking sheet. Bake for 10-12 minutes or until bubbly. Prep time: 20 minutes.

In some ways the hot crab pinwheels are similar to the hot crab dip. The real key with the pinwheels is to make sure you finely chop the onions, red peppers and parsley. It certainly makes it easier to roll up the pinwheels when the ingredients are finely chopped and the flavors are just as strong as if you roughly chopped them. This is another recipe that really is best served by making it the day before and letting the tortillas get soft overnight. Not only does it save you time by doing this but the finished pinwheels taste far better than if they are made and served immediately. The last recipe I am going to lay upon the doorstep of your kitchen, as far as appetizers go, might not seem to be so much of a finger food at first:

Turkey Confit
Use duck or chicken legs or thighs if you can't find turkey.

Legs and thighs from 1 wild turkey (you can substitute store bought chicken or duck legs)
8 cups olive oil (don't worry, it won't go to waste)
4 tablespoons of turkey sprinkle (see recipe)

Preheat oven to 200 degrees. Rub the legs and thighs liberally with the Turkey sprinkle. Place the thighs in the bottom of a dutch over (or oven safe pot). Cover the meat with the oil. The key is the meat must be covered by the oil. Place the pot in the oven and cook for 7-8 hours. The meat should pull off the bone when they are finished. Remove from the pot and shred the meat. Strain the oil and save for use in dressings or as a drizzle on pasta salad.
Prep time: 25 minutes.

Turkey Sprinkle

A great little seasoning/rub for chicken or turkey.

¼ cup coarse salt
¼ cup dried thyme
1 tablespoon garlic powder
4 tablespoons dried savory
1 tablespoon chili powder

Mix all ingredients well and store in a sealed plastic bag out of direct sunlight.
Prep time: 5 minutes.

I like to turn this confit (pronounced con-FEE) recipe into:

Turkey Confit Sandwiches

Almost like a muffaletta, too special to be called a sandwich.

4 onion buns (or plain sandwich buns)
1 lb. turkey confit (from previous recipe)
1 large sweet onion, cut into thin rings
1 large red pepper, cut into matchsticks
4 tablespoons mayonnaise
2 tablespoons sour cream
1 chipotle pepper in adobe sauce, finely chopped
½ teaspoon prepared horseradish

Place the turkey on the opened buns and add a layer of onions and peppers. In a small bowl mix the mayo, sour cream, chipotle and horseradish. Spoon over sandwiches just before serving.
Prep time: 20 minutes. Servings: 4.

I put this recipe in appetizers for the simple reason that the sandwiches make great finger foods. Build your sandwiches and then cut each one into fourths, using a toothpick to hold them together. They say that good things come to those who wait; well, this recipe is here to prove that theory in its entirety. The turkey confit is out of this world.

Confit is a method for sealing in and preserving food that has been around for hundreds of years. The French started using confit back in the day as a way to cook and preserve food and to this day if you make it, seal it up and store it in a cool place it will keep for several months. When looking at the recipe the first comment I almost always get is, "That's sure gonna be oily," although it really is not. Once the meat is finished cooking and has cooled enough to handle, drain the meat and pull it apart with your fingers. The meat should be very tender and the ligaments and tendons should fall right away from the meat. What you are left with is wonderfully flavored meat that goes great in sandwiches, soups and more. It can be frozen and used at a later date, although if you have the pot and space you can just keep it in the oil until using it. One key here is to make sure you keep the oil to use in other dishes. The meat plus the oil and other flavors leave spectacular flavored oil that can be used in dressings and for fried foods later on down the road. It's a real hole-in-one for sure.

Wow, I'm almost suffering from food coma at this point, but I must regroup and move along to many people's favorite foods. Yes my friends, we have finally made it to desserts.

Finishing Up the Tasty Way

One would think that after all the writing, posting and claims that I make of being a total foodaholic that I would be addicted to sweets. The real truth is that I very seldom eat sweets. Occasionally I tinker around in the kitchen and score a touchdown from the other end of the field with a dessert. They are not one of the things that I really cut my eye teeth on learning to cook. I feel far more comfortable with a knife and skillet in my hand then I do with the oven on and a pie plate in hand. Like most of you I have comfort zones in all things I attempt to do, and cooking is no exception. I like chopping, searing, sautéing, pan frying, and grilling. I'm not big on sticking toothpicks into things to see if they are done. All of this being said, I'm not afraid to create new dessert recipes and over the years I have done fairly well with some fantastic sweet treats. The first thing that comes to mind when I think about making a sugary selection is:

Chocolate Chip Cheeseball

Guys, impress your ladies with this easy to construct chocolate delight.

2 8 oz. packages cream cheese, softened
¾ cup butter, softened
½ teaspoon vanilla extract
½ cup fine granulated sugar
2 tablespoons brown sugar
1 cup miniature chocolate chips
¼ teaspoon cinnamon
10 Oreo cookies, crushed
½ cup chopped walnuts or pecans
1 box Honey Graham crackers

In a large mixing bowl beat cream cheese, butter and vanilla until well mixed. Add sugars and cinnamon and mix well. Stir in chocolate chips. Refrigerate for several hours (to make it easier to work with). Place the cheese on a large piece of foil or plastic wrap and shape into a ball. In a small bowl, mix Oreos and chopped nuts. Roll the cheese ball in the Oreo mixture and serve with crackers.
Prep time: 20 minutes. Servings: 8.

As you can see from my first selection, I like dessert recipes that involve using my hands. This cheeseball totally fits who I am as a cook. It's very easy to make, bursting with flavor and is a real crowd pleaser. Most people don't put cheeseball and sweet together, so it always garners some great comments and a constant barrage of, "I didn't expect that," comments from people who are expecting a salty sharp bite when they see it rolled up. The real key to this recipe is that it's just sweet enough without being overly so. Too much sugar can turn people off to a dish and the mixture of fine and brown sugars is just right to make people reach for another graham cracker. The addition of vanilla gives this treat a hint of sugar cookie goodness while the chocolate chips bring it tons of character. It tastes very similar to the filling of a cheesecake and if it had eggs or some other binder in it could be used for exactly that when placed in a graham cracker crust. Another easy to make dish is one that I recently served in a cooking class and it was without a doubt the hit of the evening:

Zucchini Bread with Raisins and Nuts

The number one hit at my vegetarian cooking class.

3 cups flour
1 teaspoon salt
1 teaspoon baking soda
1 teaspoon baking powder
2 teaspoons cinnamon
3 eggs
1 cup vegetable oil
2½ cups sugar
3 teaspoons vanilla
2 cups shredded zucchini (2 small zucchinis)
2 carrots, shredded
1 cup chopped walnuts or pecans
1 cup raisins

Preheat oven to 325 degrees. Grease 2 loaf pans and set aside. It's best to sift the dry ingredients but if you don't have the time don't worry about it. Mix the flour, salt, baking soda, baking powder and cinnamon in a mixing bowl. In another bowl beat the eggs, oil, sugar and vanilla until they are well mixed. Add the flour mixture and mix well. Fold in the zucchini, carrots, nuts and raisins. Pour into pans and bake for 50 minutes, or until a toothpick comes out clean. Allow to cool on a wire rack for several minutes before cutting.
Prep time: 25 minutes. Servings: 8.

I have already received several requests for the recipe from people who simply heard about the zucchini bread from others who attended the class. I really like the addition of carrots to this recipe, but feel free to leave them out if you don't have them on hand or don't care for them at all. The bread comes out just right on the sweetness scale and the flavors melt in your mouth. My son loves this and says unequivocally that it's the best recipe we have ever made in a cooking class. That's pretty high praise as we have made a lot of delectable dishes over the course of teaching classes. Another one of his favorites is:

Peach Pear Pie

Pears are taken to another level in this easy to make pie.

2 fresh pears, skinned, cored and sliced
2 fresh peaches, skinned and sliced (or 1 can peach slices)
2 tablespoons butter
1 8 oz. container unflavored yogurt
½ cup chopped walnuts
¼ cup raisins
½ teaspoon cinnamon
½ teaspoon vanilla flavoring
¾ cup brown sugar
2 teaspoons cornstarch
3 tablespoons milk
2 refrigerated pie crusts

Preheat over to 425 degrees. Place the butter in a large skillet on medium heat. Add the pear slices and cook for 5 minutes. Flip pears and add peach slices. Meanwhile in a small bowl, mix yogurt, cinnamon, vanilla and brown sugar. Fold in walnuts and raisins. Add to skillet and bring to a simmer. In a small cup, mix the milk and cornstarch. Slowly add the milk mixture to the skillet, stirring often until the peaches thicken. Remove the skillet from heat. Line a pie pan (preferably a glass pan) with one pie crust. Spoon the peach and pear filling into the crust and cover with the second crust. Trim edges and flute. Place into the over and cook for 30 minutes or until top is nicely browned.

Prep time: 20 minutes. Servings: 8.

Back a few paragraphs I talked about how I didn't care for oven cooking sweets a whole lot. I never said I couldn't do it however, and this recipe is a testament to exactly that. The pears really show through in this recipe and sautéing them in the skillet before baking them gets rid of the graininess that makes so many people not like fresh pairs. Peaches are a natural pairing here and if you can get your hands on fresh ones, this pie really shines. When I make this pie my wife and son always help by putting the crusts on the pie and making unique shapes with the excess crust. They then place the designs on top of the pie before it's cooked. They have made circles, stars and more and it makes the finished pie look as good as it tastes. Don't worry if you are not a big baker, as this pie is very easy to make. There's no requirement for a baking PhD here, but you wouldn't know it once the family gets into it and starts telling you how great it is. The thick, gooey center is a perfect match to the flaky crusts and the yogurt and cinnamon make this filling unlike tradition fruit pies. Here's another recipe that came from time spent in the kitchen with family:

Easy Fruit Salad

*Using canned fruit makes this recipe easier
to throw together at the last minute.*

2 ripe bananas, sliced into ½" pieces
1 large apple, peeled, cored and cut into ½" pieces
2 kiwi fruits, peeled and cut into ¼" pieces
1 cup fresh strawberries, cut into ½" pieces
1 cup peach slices (canned is fine), cut into ½" pieces
1 cup pineapple tidbits, drained
Juice from 2 limes
¼ cup sugar
1 cup granola

Mix all fruits. Squeeze limes over fruit. Add sugar and toss to
coat. Divide into bowls and sprinkle with granola.
Prep time: 20 minutes. Servings: 8.

One day we were sitting around my mom's kitchen talking
about how our weeks at work had been, when the subject of fruit
salads came up. We talked about things we liked and things we
didn't like and decided to make one with all the things we loved.
The Easy Fruit salad above is the result of that time spent just
talking back and forth and enjoying one another's company. The
lime juice melds with the sugar to make the most wonderful sweet
sauce, and the acid from the limes really serves to keep your fruit
from turning brown. With the availability of fresh fruit at your
local supermarket in this day and age this recipe can pretty much
be made any time of year, with just a substitution or two for what's
fresh at that particular time. While we were at it that day we took
the fruit salad a bit further and came up with:

Delectable Fruit Salad

Not just a plain old fruit salad, this one zings.

2 cups fresh raspberries
2 cups fresh blackberries
2 cups fresh blueberries
2 cups strawberries, cut into ½" pieces
2 large bananas, cut into ½" pieces
1 cup marshmallow cream
4 oz. cream cheese, softened
½ teaspoon vanilla flavoring
1 teaspoon Amaretto

In a large bowl mix all fruits lightly, being careful not to crush them. In a small mixing bowl, beat marshmallow cream and cream cheese until smooth. Add vanilla and Amaretto. Mix well. Gently fold into mixed fruit.
Prep time: 25 minutes. Servings: 8.

The title of fruit salad might be the same in both of those recipes but that's where the similarities end. This delectable fruit salad is just that, delectable. It's creamy and smooth and just sparkles when served over pound cake or angel food cake. It is good stand alone, but don't underestimate its ability to take a plain ole cake to the next level. It's wonderful made up and put along side cakes on the dessert table. The real difference is the two is that the Easy Fruit Salad can be made the day before and it holds up well, while the Delectable Fruit Salad should be made at most an hour before serving. As the juices of the fruits leach out they tend to water down the creamy sauce and make it runny. Its peak serving is when the sauce is thick and creamy, basically freshly made. One dish that can be made a couple of hours ahead of time and allowed to stand by is:

Slow Cooker Brownie Fudge Pudding

For all the slow cooker fans out there, this one is a home run!

1 cup flour
2 teaspoons baking powder
¾ cup sugar
4 tablespoons cocoa
½ cup milk
2 tablespoons butter
1 teaspoon vanilla
¾ cup packed brown sugar
2 tablespoons
2 boiling water

In a large bowl combine the flour, baking powder, sugar and cocoa. Stir well. In a separate bowl combine the milk, butter and vanilla. Stir into the flour mixture. Spread into a greased slow cooker. In a small bowl combine the brown sugar and cocoa. Add boiling water and mix well. Pour over the batter in the slow cooker slowly. Cover and cook on high for 2 hours. Check for doneness with a toothpick. Spoon into bowls and serve with ice cream or bread pudding.
Prep time: 20 minutes. Servings: 10.

Before you start to think brownies here, let me say something. This pudding is going to render out to a fairly thin consistency, but that in no way makes it any less delicious then regular old brownies or pudding. It's best when served over something, with vanilla pudding being my favorite and apple pie, yes apple pie, coming in a close second. For those of you who love your slow cookers this may not be something that you think of as being a common dish for that preparation but it comes out awesome. Chocolaty, gooey and sweet, what could be better than that and the preparation is simple as can be. If you want to serve it directly from the slow cooker, tear an angel food cake into pieces and serve on a plate beside the slow cooker with some fondue sticks and let people dip it themselves.

It's a real knockout and no one will believe you didn't spend half a day getting it ready. While you may spend some time getting it put together, one recipe that doesn't take any time at all to whip up just so happens to be at the top of my dessert favorites list:

Biscuits with Fried Apples

Use up those apples that have been sitting in the bowl for a week.

4 large apples (Gala or the like) peeled, seeded and cut into ½" cubes
4 tablespoons real butter
4 tablespoons sugar
¾ teaspoon ground cinnamon
1 container refrigerated biscuits, cooked according to package directions
1 pint heavy cream, whipped
1 teaspoon sugar

In a large sauce pan melt butter over medium heat. Add apples and cook, stirring frequently for 8 minutes, or until apples are tender. Add sugar and cinnamon. Continue to cook for 1 minute, to dissolve sugar. Cut a biscuit in half, spoon apples over biscuits and top with whipped cream.
Prep time: 15 minutes. Servings 6.

Apples and frying, now there's two things that go together better than peanut butter and jelly. When I was a little whipper snapper, I can remember having fried apple pies that my grandmother made. I have never made them myself, but the gist of it was they would dry apples during the summer when they were plentiful and later on, usually in the winter, they would take them out, reconstitute them and fry them inside a crust. Again, I have never made them, but I sure have eaten a bunch of them and the fried apples in this recipe remind me of those pies and those days way back when. As I said earlier, I don't remember a lot about my childhood, but I sure do remember those tasty treats and in many ways what I have done here is created an open faced version of them. Topping the fresh cooked biscuits with the piping hot apples causes the whipped cream to melt down onto the plate, leaving you some liquid to soak up with the remaining biscuits. My grandpa used to call this "sopping up" the liquid, and boy would he love this if he were alive today. I can see him right now swinging that biscuit back and forth across his plate gathering up every last bit of goodness. His plate would be cleaner than before we put the food on it. It harkens me back to a different place when life was slower, family and friends saw more of one another and food was a gathering point for all of us.

Back when I was in college I took a class on the History of Rock and Roll. No, I'm not going to type away and try to impress you with my knowledge of Elvis Presley and Paul Anka, but one thing really sticks out in my mind from that class. Each time we would meet, the professor would say we were going on a sojourn. My friends, we have come to the end of our culinary sojourn as far as recipes go. I hope you and your families enjoy them as much as my family and I have through the years. Now it's time for some tips and tactics from the man who has cut himself so many times his fingers curl up involuntarily when they see a knife – me!

There's Got to Be an Easier Way

Sometimes it seems that no matter what you do there's just no easy way to do anything. Pots and lids slip from your grasp, pans are always hotter than you think they are going to be, no surface is ever flat and knives cut you more than they do your foods. It happens to everyone at some point in time. I am not going to come on here and claim to be a witch doctor that can save you from those things happening to you; what I can do, however, is offer you some tips that I have found, usually through error and not trial, that really save you time and effort.

1.   The first tip I always give no matter who I am talking to and where I am is simply to keep you knives sharp. This may seem odd to some people that having a sharp knife would be a tip to help keep you from getting cut, but that is entirely the case. A sharp knife takes less effort to cut with and effort will save your fingertips. When you don't have to hack and saw whatever it is you are cutting, you are safer as a result. There are tons of good knife sharpeners for not much money. The one I use costs less than 30 dollars, and is small enough that it can be used in almost any situation. My 11-year-old son sharpens with it just as good as I do. Look for one that has slots for serrated and plain blades if you use serrated knives. Read the instructions for safe use as cutting yourself while sharpening a knife is worse than cutting yourself with it when you are actually using it. After you have

it down, keep your knives sharp with it. It's much easier to keep a knife sharp than to sharpen it from scratch each time. I sharpen mine about once every two weeks if that gives you an idea of how often to sharpen them.

2. The second tip that I usually give out is to keep oven mitts close at hand. Beyond cuts the most often injury that I hear about is burns. Typically, burns occur when you don't have an oven mitt close at hand and attempt to grab something hot with a towel or a similar object that was not designed to take extreme heat. If you have mitts near by you are far more apt to use them.

3. I spoke earlier about burning my hand on the stove top when I was younger. Many stoves now have lights that stay on as long as a surface is hot. Try to get in the habit of looking at the stove before ever placing anything, be it your hands or food, on the surface. This is easy to forget. Unless you get in the habit of looking at the lights, it's almost impossible to remind yourself each time. Oddly enough, you can hurt your food just as bad by placing a pan on a burner that you didn't think was hot. The next thing you know it's scalded to the bottom and ruined.

4. Get your kids into the kitchen with you as soon as they are interested. When my son was little, my wife and I let him cook with us whenever he wanted. We gave him a spoon and a butter knife so he couldn't hurt himself too badly, I guess, and let him go at it. To this day he loves to cook and is a very good cook in his own right. He's not afraid to tackle any kitchen job and makes a mean roux for a little fella.

5. Keep an apron handy. Very seldom do I wear an apron when people are over or when I have the food prepared, but nothing makes it easier to stay clean while you are preparing food than an apron. It's easy on, easy off, and will keep your Sunday go-to-meeting clothes in presentable shape. Most aprons also have pockets which are great for keeping salt shakers, pepper grinders, spatulas and more close at hand. In a lot of ways it's like the oven mitt; if it's close it gets used. Out of sight, out of mind.

6. One thing that I always try to do while cooking is keep my dishes washed as I go. If I use a pot and I move the ingredients to another pot, or to a mixing bowl, I wash the pot immediately. Be careful that the pots and pans are not too hot prior to putting them in the water, but keeping them washed sure makes for a lot less stress later on in the evening. Follow the cleaning instructions that came with your pots and pans to make sure you are not using soaps or abrasives that might scratch them. If possible, wash and reuse the same pot for different steps of a recipe; this way you use less pots or bowls, less water and it's easier on you in the end. Also keep in mind that many items – premium knives come to mind – should not be put in the dishwasher. They are best washed by hand.

7. Prep prep prep. I can sum it up that easily. The more prep work you can do ahead of time, the easier it will be on you and the less stress you will have come time to serve your meal. I always include stress lessening tips in all my presentations, as through the years I have found this to be one of the main reasons people don't make certain dishes. Time spent preparing and cooking food should be as enjoyable as possible. It can even be fun if you plan things before you dive into them. Make it so that you do as much as you can in the days leading up to the dinner. Several years back I started a Wild Game Supper at our church. The first year there were 66 people in attendance and within six years it has grown to more than 300. The real key to feeding this many people, in a timely and efficient manner, is planning. You can't start getting things ready the day before and expect it to be stress free. I would typically start tying up loose ends and working on prepping foods a week or more in advance of the dinner. Anything that could be precooked was precooked, all my fry dredge was made during the weeks leading up to the dinner. I was making forty pounds of dredge at a time, and items that needed to be cut up were chopped and frozen so that all I had to do was thaw out prior to cooking. All these things led to an easy day once the dinner arrived. Basically we would assemble, heat up and fry items prior to the arrival of the guests and that was it. All the other work would have already been done.

8. Always keep thaw times in mind when dealing with meats. It's always best not to try to force meat to thaw. What I mean by forcing it to thaw is microwaving, putting it in water and the like. Not only does it facilitate the growth of bacteria and other unwanted pests, it can affect the flavor and tenderness of the meat. According

to its size, a frozen turkey may need to be placed in the refrigerator three or four days prior to cooking to get fully thawed. If you forget, it's best to head to the store and buy a fresh one rather than force thaw the one in the fridge. Leave it for use later on.

9. Don't cut tender fruits and vegetables too soon as they will wilt and turn brown in the amount of time it takes you to get everything else ready. Bananas and avocados are perfect examples of this, although there are many more I could list. It's best to cut them just before using, and if you are going to be held up any time at all, use a citrus juice, lemon or lime, to keep them from browning. The acid will slow the process of browning giving you extra time to get everything ready. Just squeeze the juice from a lemon, lime or orange into a bowl and toss the foods with the juice. It will make a huge difference in the appearance of the dish.

10. One question that I seemingly get at all stops is how to better present food. The one tip that I can really say has helped me a ton through the years is to have two colors of serving dishes and bowls. Having a dark, blue, black or red and a light colored set really allows you to show every recipe in its best light. The artichoke dip, for instance, tends to look washed out if served in a white bowl or dish, where-as if you serve it in blue or another dark color it looks fabulous. Barbecued ribs look best when presented on a light colored background. Keep in mind what the finished color will be and adjust your serving dishes accordingly.

11. Try to keep a few basic foods around most all the time. My list of foods that you can expect to find in my kitchen 360 days a year reads like this: white and black pepper, garlic powder, chili powder, ground up chilies (both mild and hot), lemons, limes, roasted peppers, canned artichokes, tomato sauce and paste, several varieties of beans including green and lima, ground beef or chicken, Italian sausage links, hot sauce, shredded cheddar cheese, cream cheese, milk, whole wheat bread, whole wheat pasta, brown rice and a selection of fresh, dried or freeze dried herbs. This list may seem a little long, except when you put it all together you could just about carry it in one big bag. These essentials allow me whip up a dip on short notice, throw together a casserole for dinner or create a fantastic side dish in a matter of minutes, without having to make a trip to the grocery.

Add or subtract items that you don't like but keep a fair amount of ones that you do on hand at all times. It saves money from that urge to run out and grab fast food when you can throw something together in your pajamas.

12. Keep a selection of different size pots and pans on hand. It's a real pain to have to use a huge pot for just a small bit of ingredients especially when it comes time to wash it. Having a good selection on hand allows you to use a pot or pan that fits what you are trying to do. Look at it like this: if you can help it, you don't use a heavy winter coat for cool weather, you use a jacket. Having both allows you to be comfortable, just like having different size pots and pans allows you to be comfortable in the kitchen.

13. Roast your own peppers, dry your own herbs and save yourself some money. Roasting peppers is as easy as putting them on a grill or under the broiler until the skins blister and char, rotating them so that all sides get charred. Remove them and place in a large plastic bag for a few minutes. Remove them from the bag, peel the skins off and freeze or store in jars filled with olive oil. Herbs can be just as easily dried by hanging them in a cold dark place or simply place them in a plastic bag and freeze. They will be perfect for using later on and the only investment you had in them was a couple of dollars for seeds and a planter or two.

14. Forget that your grill and your stove have a high setting. Literally, I mean forget it. I have never cooked anything on my grill or on my stove that needed to be cooked on high other than boiling water. That's it. If you forget high and remember medium you will have much less heartache in the kitchen and your entire house will smell much better due to the lack of burned foods.

15. Anytime you know you are going to fry something, plan ahead. Make your breading up ahead of time and most importantly go ahead and dredge your meat or vegetables an hour or so (even longer if you have time) and put them in the refrigerator. Breading them and letting them sit allows the breading to adhere better and will lessen the chances that it falls off while cooking.

16. Use a wash prior to dipping in the dredge. I like buttermilk or heavy cream (I like heavy cream on most everything as a matter of fact) but eggs work equally well. Use a medium size mixing bowl to hold your wash, dip your food into it, then into the dredge and lay it on a plate. Sprinkle some of the dredge over the layer before you place another layer on top so they don't stick together. When coupled with allowing extra time, the wash will really make a significant difference in how much breading stays on the food.

17. Always make sure that your oil is hot enough to fry before adding in your food. The key here is knowing how hot the oil is prior to putting in your food. If you're using an electric skillet or wok there is a temperature setting on it, but if not, you need to use a thermometer and find out what the temperature is just before you add your meat or vegetables. Think of it like this: if you want your oil to fry at 350 degrees and that is exactly where the temperature is sitting, once you add cold food to it the temperature is going to drop. In the case of frying an entire turkey, the temperature may drop as much as 40 or 50 degrees when the bird is placed in the oil. Now instead of frying at 350 your bird is stewing at 300. Get that oil a little hotter than your ideal cooking temperature before you add the food, then adjust the heat after a few minutes when it's settled a little more.

18. Do not limit yourself in what you think you can fry. Almost everything can be fried and still produce an edible meal. Heck, at the State Fairs now they fry butter. Literally they bread butter and fry it. I have fried chocolate, Twinkies, marshmallows and more. Look outside the norm when it comes to frying and you just might discover something great.

19. Whenever you are using herbs, be they fresh or dried, and you only want the flavor without the herbs showing up in your dish, put the herbs in cheesecloth or a coffee filter, wrap it up and secure with kitchen twine. This is especially true of using rosemary, thyme and other herbs that tend to have tough leaves and stems. Once you've finished using the herbs remove the packet and discard. Most herbs will need to be heated for several minutes to render the flavor into your dish. Some, like bay leaves, need more time so keep in mind what you are using and go by the recommendation on the recipe you are using.

20. A non-reactive bowl is one that won't react with the ingredients to alter the flavor of your recipe. Some foods that are highly acidic can react with certain metal pans (such as copper) and give your foods a metallic taste. Examples of non-reactive bowls are stainless steel, glass and heavy duty plastics. When it comes to figuring out whether or not plastic bowls are reactive, keep this in mind, if it stains after having food in it, that is a sign of it being reactive.

21. Don't try too hard to emulate a picture you see in a cookbook. I debated whether or not to include pictures in this cookbook for the single reason that often times when a dish doesn't come out looking like the picture in the book, I feel it's a failure in some respects. You are not always going to find the exact ingredients called for in a recipe which will no doubt affect the end result looks of your creation. In addition, some of the pictures in these books may have been taken under ideal conditions that cannot be replicated in the typical home kitchen. If your recipe tastes good you did a fine job. Period.

22. Appetizers and desserts tend to be harder to figure as far as number of servings go. One tip that I go by is to figure on dip or snack food for every eight people you are feeding. You will need to adjust this slightly according to how much food you are serving for your main course. If you have a large, heavy dinner such as fried chicken, cut back on your appetizers. Vice versa, if you are serving a light soup for your main course, it's good to have a selection of appetizers, cheeses and such so no one leaves hungry. Always keep this in mind: the true definition of a bad party is one in which people left hungry.

So, my friends, it seems we are finally at the end of this great journey. All of these recipes, and stories for that matter, represent stages in my cooking life, and I hope that you can find at least a few that will serve to bring your families and friends together. I have often said, "If it takes food to get my family together, then by golly, I'll cook every day for the rest of my life." After all, Family, Friends and Food are what life is all about.

About the Author

Way back in the days when kids played outside all day and the parents didn't worry, we were in a different time, not only in our family lives, but food-wise as well. Restaurants were rarely ate at with most families preferring to cook and eat at home. Home cooking, so to speak, is what Shawn grew up eating and is the basis for most of his cooking today. Shawn can fondly remember the days of fried chicken, pinto beans, cornbread and kale  greens steaming in bowls on the table. There were always angel food and cheese cakes around for the after dinner treats. Growing up in Kentucky gave Shawn an appreciation for the great bounty of foods that we have available to us.

As a child, Shawn found himself to be a serious eater. Many times when answering the question of how he got to where he is today, Shawn gives the simple but true answer, "I had to learn to cook because I loved to eat." That statement defines Shawn's culinary journey. Shawn has always been driven to cook, to explore the limits of food and the preparations that make food such a part of daily life. Growing up on a farm, Shawn came to appreciate the work involved in making a Sunday dinner, canning vegetables and feeding a crew of people.

Since the mid-90's when Shawn's wife and he graduated from the University of Louisville, and were married, they have lived on a farm in Trimble County and grown many of their own vegetables, herbs and fruits. Since his first job in the restaurant industry over 25 years ago, Shawn has worked in many different restaurant positions, including fast food and up scale dining as well as working in sales and owning his own business. This love of cooking is what drove Shawn to start Keeton in the Kitchen.

Kristen Snyder of *The News Democrat* states, "Shawn Keeton's life has been a 'Culinary Expedition.' Keeton's website also has weekly tips, recipes and any updates about the various projects Keeton is involved in." What began as a website to provide tips and ideas for friends morphed into a blog, and many other online endeavors as well as Keeton in the Kitchen television.

Keeton in the Kitchen television is a look into Shawn's kitchen; a chance to see how Shawn prepares and serves his dishes in both an indoor and outdoor setting. The cooking show has allowed Shawn to grow in his cooking and presentation style and represents the next chapter in his cooking journey through the teaching of cooking classes. Shawn began teaching cooking classes as a way to give back to all of those who have supported him through his cooking endeavors.

"He's a very funny guy. He's so creative and energetic when he does the cooking program. He's great with people and with cooking," says Mandy Parker. The classes have been taught in a variety of settings to a multitude of diverse groups ranging from annual retreats to women's groups. Shawn also features a variety of seminars with topics ranging from knife skills to getting picky children to eat better. Shawn continues to grow his repertoire of cooking and presenting skills as well as spreading the word of Keeton in the Kitchen television.

Shawn continues to work on Keeton in the Kitchen television with a planned release of Thanksgiving 2010. Additionally Shawn can be found teaching cooking classes as well as blogging on his website, www.keetoninthekitchen.com. Shawn can also be found on his Facebook site, Keeton in the Kitchen, as well as on other types of digital media such as MySpace and can be contacted online at shawn@keetoninthekitchen.com.

"You'll have to cook two to three meals a day for the rest of your life," Keeton says. "You might as well enjoy it."

Recipe Index